TWENTIETH CENTURY INTERPRETATIONS
OF

WUTHERING
HEIGHTS

A Collection of Critical Essays

Edited by

THOMAS A. VOGLER

Prentice-Hall, Inc. *Englewood Cliffs, N. J.*
A SPECTRUM BOOK

Current printing (last number):
10 9 8 7 6 5 4 3 2

Contents

Introduction

by Thomas A. Vogler

The Life

Emily Brontë's father was born Patrick Branty or Bruntee, one of the ten children of a peasant farmer in northern Ireland. He began earning his own living at an early age, first as a blacksmith, then as a linen weaver. At sixteen he became headmaster of a small village school, and later was a private tutor to the sons of a Methodist clergyman. He saved what money he could until, at twenty-five, he was able to enter Cambridge University as a sizar, receiving financial assistance on the grounds of poverty. Four years later he took his degree and was ordained a clergyman in the Church of England. He wrote and published two volumes of poems, two narratives, and several pamphlets and sermons, none of which has received any attention, either on its own slim merits or as a source of influence on his daughters. In all this, he stands out as a man of remarkable will and stamina, driving himself to overcome great hardships and achieve ambitious goals. After this first prolonged burst of effort, however, he seems to have settled down to a quiet existence as a country curate. His expectations may or may not have been satisfied. At any rate, his strivings ceased.

In 1812, while curate at Hartshead, and in the midst of his writing career, Patrick married Maria Branwell. By 1820 they had six children (Maria, born 1813; Elizabeth, 1815; Charlotte, 1816; Patrick Branwell, 1817; Emily Jane, 1818; Anne, 1820) and were settled in the parsonage at Haworth, a remote northern village in Yorkshire. Mrs. Brontë died in 1821, and the older daughters, Maria and Elizabeth, died in 1825 as the result of rigid discipline and discomfort in a private boarding school.

At this point, the location and membership in the family circle was stabilized, with Mrs. Brontë's sister taking over as housekeeper. The four children were highly imaginative, had read widely and were interested in imitating what they had read. The stimulus

which first started them writing was a set of wooden soldiers which
the Reverend Brontë brought home in June, 1826. Around these
soldiers the children created an elaborate imaginary world called
Angria, with a history, a geography, newspapers, philosophers,
poets, lovers, and statesmen. For five years they worked together to
put this world on paper, not writing about it, but creating the
thing itself, the poems and speeches and essays of the people in it.
In 1831, when Charlotte left for school at Roe Head, Emily rebelled
against the leadership of her brother Branwell and began building
her own world of Gondal, which she worked on with her younger
sister, Anne. Although Gondal was located in the South Pacific,
it was much more like Yorkshire than the more idyllic Angria; and
the characters in it lived and suffered lives of a more elemental and
tragic nature. Except for three brief interruptions (a period at
school, a few months as a governess in 1837, and eight months at
a private school in France in 1842), Emily spent the next fourteen
years in Haworth parsonage, helping with the housework, taking
long walks on the moorland, reading and continuing to create the
open-ended world of Gondal. For the tone of what her life was
like during this long period, we have two remarkable documents
written to be opened in the future. The first is from November,
1834:

> This morning Branwell went down to Mr. Driver's and brought
> news that Sir Robert Peel was going to be invited to stand for Leeds.
> Anne and I have been peeling apples for Charlotte to make a pudding
> and for Aunt's . . . Charlotte said she made puddings perfectly and
> she . . . of quick but limited intellect. Tabby said just now Come
> Anne pillo-putate (i.e., pill a potate). Aunt has come into the kitchen
> just now and said Where are your feet Ann Anne answered On the
> floor Aunt. Papa opened the parlour door and gave Branwell a
> letter saying Here Branwell read this and show it to your Aunt and
> Charlotte. The Gondals are discovering the interior of Gaaldine.
> Sally Mosely is washing in the back kitchin.
> It is past twelve o'clock Anne and I have not tided ourselves done
> our bed work, or done our lessons and we want to go out to play.
> We are going to have for dinner Boiled Beef, Turnips, potatoes
> and apple pudding. The kitchin is in a very untidy state. Anne and
> I have not our music lesson which consists of a *b major* Taby said
> on my putting a pen in her face Ya pitter pottering there instead of
> pilling a potate. I answered O dear, O dear, O dear I will derectly
> With that I get up, take a knife and begin pilling. Finished pilling
> the potatoes Papa going to walk Mr. Sunderland expected.
> Anne and I say I wonder what we shall be like and what we shall

be and where we shall be if all goes well, in the year 1874—in which
year I shall be in my 57th year. Anne will be in her 55th year Branwell
will be going on in his 58th year and Charlotte in her 59th year.
Hoping we shall all be well at that time. We close our paper.

Emily and Anne.[1]

The conclusion to the other letter, dated July 30, 1841, reveals the
same simultaneous involvement with the people and life around
her and her private world of Gondal:

> It is Friday evening, near 9 o'clock—wild rainy weather. I am
> seated in the dining-room, having just concluded tidying our desk
> boxes, writing this document. Papa is in the parlour—aunt upstairs in
> her room. She has been reading *Blackwood's Magazine* to papa.
> Victoria and Adelaide are ensconced in the peat-house. Keeper is in
> the kitchen—Hero in his cage. We are all stout and hearty, as I
> hope is the case with Charlotte, Branwell, and Anne. . . .
> The *Gondaland* are at present in a threatening state, but there is
> no open rupture as yet. All the princes and princesses of the Royalty
> are at the Palace of Instruction. I have a good many books on hands,
> but I am sorry to say that as usual I make small progress with any.
> However, I have just made a new regularity paper! and I must *verb
> sap* to do great things. And now I close, sending from far an ex-
> hortation of courage, boys! courage, to exiled and harassed Anne,
> wishing she was here.

Earlier in this letter she is wondering "whether we shall still be
dragging on in our present condition or established to our hearts'
content" when it is opened. She hopes that their debts will be paid
off and that "It will be a fine warm summer evening, very different
from this bleak look-out." Part of the bleakness of this second
paper comes from her increased age. Now a young lady of twenty-
three, she had begun to realize that she had few prospects in life
except those of becoming a governess or starting her own private
boarding school. She knew from experience that she would not like
either.

The first great change in Emily's life since the advent of the
toy soldiers came in 1845, when Charlotte discovered some of the
Gondal poems and proposed that the sisters enter the public world

---

[1] The incoherence of this document is the incoherence of life, which insists on
mixing and combining different levels of reality in given moments of time. Its
unity is in the lively, humorous mind of the girl who is aware of the differences
yet fully capable of combining them into one total perception. Joyce begins his
A Portrait of the Artist with a comparable (though deliberately more infantile)
state of consciousness.

of authorship. They quickly put together a small volume of poems and each of them began a novel, thinking that fiction would be more profitable than verse. Their first published work combined the poems of Charlotte, Emily, and Anne under the pseudonyms of Currer, Ellis, and Acton Bell. Although it received three mildly favorable reviews, the volume sold only two copies. Unbowed by this failure, which cost them fifty pounds in publication expenses, the sisters continued work on their novels as an avenue to fame and fortune. Within a year Emily had written *Wuthering Heights*, Anne had written *Agnes Grey*, and Charlotte, *The Professor*. The turn to fiction, and the rapidity and skill of their efforts, are not as miraculous as they might seem at first. For twenty years, the girls had been writing, filling hundreds of pages with microscopic hand-printing. On the public side, the country was experiencing an insatiable demand for fiction, without which the sisters might not have ventured into print or been accepted by their publishers.[2]

As it was, Charlotte's *Professor* was not accepted for publication, but she received an encouraging note from a publisher, asking for a longer novel, which prompted her to finish *Jane Eyre*. This novel was in fact published first because of delay on the part of Emily and Anne's publisher. It was an immediate success, so much so that when *Wuthering Heights* and *Agnes Grey* came out two months later, the publisher openly insinuated that Acton and Ellis Bell were other names for the now popular Currer Bell. In spite of this ploy, the novels were not so well-received as *Jane Eyre*. *Wuthering Heights* was condemned in a number of reviews. Mr. Bell was characterized as "dogged, brutal and morose," his work "rude and unfinished," an "unnatural" tale of "human degradation" in which all the characters were "hateful" and "contemptible." In all the notice it received, only one review was entirely favorable.

Much to Emily's dismay, Anne and Charlotte went to London and revealed the true identities of the Messrs. Bell. Before notoriety could set in, however, Emily died of consumption in December, 1848, to be followed a few months later by Anne. Branwell too had died during the fall of 1848. Charlotte went on to publish two more novels and to marry before she died in 1855. The Reverend Patrick Brontë lived quietly on to the age of eighty-four, and died in 1861.

[2] Cf. Kathleen Tillotson, *Novels of the Eighteen-Forties* (Oxford, 1965), for an excellent discussion of the literary climate in Britain during this period. She credits Sir Walter Scott with having purified the unsavory reputation of the novel (pp. 15–16).

These facts, in brief, are the framework on which the many legends of the three Brontë sisters have been woven. In a life that would be severe and oppressive by our standards, they seem to have achieved a kind of contentment that was genuine. What we know of Emily is that she was a quiet and private person, extremely self-sufficient, fond of solitary walks on the moorland, a hard-working housekeeper and a prolific writer. In addition, the "great things" to which she dedicated herself in the 1841 paper came to pass; for it was her novel, not the more immediately popular *Jane Eyre*, which in the long run came to be considered the Brontë's greatest achievement.

Wuthering Heights

An introduction, especially to a collection of others' views, should not offer a pre-emptive explanation of the work under consideration. Ideally, it should indicate only what kind of work is being dealt with, and what it is about. From there, the reader can go on to make his own discoveries and to enjoy his own experience of reading and interpreting. In *Wuthering Heights*, however, it is precisely these questions that are the most difficult, and the most widely debated. Much of what is written on the book tries to simplify its complexity by seizing only a part of it, and claiming that part as the key which unlocks in some magic fashion all the mysteries and ambiguities of the text. What is needed is clearly a move in the opposite direction, towards recognition that the book, in its ambiguity, demands continued rereading, and reflection on the most basic question of how it should be read. Any final view of the novel must be arrived at after immersion in the substance and complexities of the work itself; it must grow organically out of the experience of reading the work, and be related to it at every point.

If we resist our tendency to look past or through the characters at what they might represent, either in symbolic or allegorical form, we see something not unlike the realistic novel of the late eighteenth and early nineteenth centuries. It is rooted in concrete and specific images of reality; it is set at a particular place, and the action occurs during a clearly specified interval of time. Whatever its meaning, then, there is an implicit assumption that it will be referable to the characters and places in the book, even though it may transcend that limited level of reality.

One way a writer can convince a reader that there is some significance lurking in all the events of a work is by giving direct signals, letting him know that the structure of his work is deliberately patterned on some theory or model of reality. Such signals range from the direct statement of an allegorist like Dante to the selective "natural" imagery of a novelist like Dreiser. But in such cases, we know that there is a Truth (Christianity for Dante, Darwinian survival of the fittest for Dreiser) that binds together all the parts of their work.

Another way is to create characters who are hungry for meaning, for a context that will clarify the significance of their identities and experiences, and then to put these characters into a world where there are no guidelines except what they themselves can discover. Emily Brontë is similar to Melville, Conrad, and James in her emphasis on this kind of meaning. Everything is contained in the mind of Lockwood, who begins the novel with his curious poking about the Heights, entering it, "inspecting the penetralium," trying to understand and interpret what he sees—even catching himself making mistakes in his first impression of Heathcliff ("I'm running on too fast—I bestow my own attributes over liberally on him"). He ends up thoroughly confused, and turns to Nelly Dean for explanations.

Nelly is like Lockwood, both in her need to understand and in having staked her comprehension of life on the objective level of empirical reality. She lives in a world of things and of rational, causal explanations of events:

> I smelt the rich scent of the heating spices; and admired the shining kitchen utensils, the polished clock, decked in holly, the silver mugs ranged on a tray ready to be filled with mulled ale for supper; and, above all, the speckless purity of my particular care—the scoured and well-swept floor.
>
> I gave due inward applause to every object, and, then, I remembered how old Earnshaw used to come in when all was tidied, and call me a cant lass, and slip a shilling into my hand as a Christmas box . . . (Ch. VII)

Here she is secure, in control, and being rewarded for her control. Anything not reducible to this level of existence is, for both Nelly and Lockwood, a threat to their hold on reality:

> "Is he a ghoul, or a vampire?" I mused. I had read of such hideous, incarnate demons. And then, I set myself to reflect, how I had tended him in infancy; and watched him grow to youth; and followed him almost through his whole course; and what absurd nonsense it was to yield to that sense of horror.

"But, where did he come from, the little dark thing, harboured by a good man to his bane?" muttered superstition, as I dozed into unconsciousness. And I began, half dreaming, to weary myself with imagining some fit parentage for him; and repeating my waking meditations. . . . all I can remember is, being exceedingly vexed at having the task of dictating an inscription for his monument, and consulting the sexton about it; and, as he had no surname, and we could not tell his age, we were obliged to content ourselves with the single word, "Heathcliff." That came true; we were. If you enter the kirkyard, you'll read on his headstone, only that, and the date of his death.

Dawn restored me to common sense. I rose, and went into the garden, as soon as I could see, to ascertain if there were any footmarks under his window. There were none. (Ch. XXXIV)

This passage shows how "common sense" works, what its results are, and why it is so important. Lurking behind "common sense" is the "sense of horror" provoked by anything not readily explicable in its terms. The horror must be "absurd nonsense," the pastime of children and the superstitious, because it is too threatening to entertain seriously. For Nelly, the proper use of the supernatural is the kind of play we see in her songs and tales. Lockwood refers to Catherine's hexing of Joseph as a "kind of dreary fun," and is himself given to joking about ghosts. The price paid for this rational security is a reduction of the scope of vision to what is before one's eyes. Ultimately, the only meaning to be derived from Heathcliff's story is a "single word . . . only that, and the date of his death." When Nelly describes Heathcliff a few paragraphs later, with his eyes fixed on "something within two yards' distance," whatever he is staring at must be a "fancied object" only, for it cannot truly exist in Nelly's world.

Lockwood's mind reveals the same pattern, and an even more extreme example of the same need. He is terrified at his dreamlike experience in Chapter III, reporting himself in "a frenzy of fright," trembling and perspiring. Even though he can "explain" the dream away, as "an impression which personified itself when I had my imagination no longer under control," he cannot sleep more that night. The last discussion between Nelly and Lockwood is almost directly about this matter. Nelly reports having seen the little boy with his lambs, crying:

"They's Heathcliff, and a woman, yonder, under t'nab," he blubbered, "un' Aw darnut pass 'em."

I saw nothing; but neither the sheep nor he would go on, so I bid him take the road lower down.

He probably raised the phantoms from thinking, as he traversed
the moors alone, on the nonsense he had heard his parents and
companions repeat—yet still, I don't like being out in the dark,
now—and I don't like being left by myself in this grim house—I cannot help it, I shall be glad when they leave it, and shift to the Grange!
(Ch. XXXIV)

Nelly's "probably," and her honest admission of nervousness sum-
marize nicely where she stands. She is committed to controlling her
"fancy" or "imagination," the two names used in the book for the
source of superstitious "nonsense." But she knows that her control
is not perfect. Lockwood, on the other hand, responds with a joke
about ghosts moving into the Heights, and goes on to look at the
graves:

I lingered round them, under that benign sky; watched the moths
fluttering among the heath and hare-bells; listened to the soft wind
breathing through the grass; and wondered how anyone could ever
imagine unquiet slumbers, for the sleepers in that quiet earth.

These final lines give many readers the assurance of an achieved
peace for Cathy and Heathcliff. Their content, however, seems more
relevant to Lockwood. With his dream-vision long forgotten, everything looks quiet to him; he can't imagine any real ghosts, or any
afterlife except a quiet slumber, so he looks at what is before his eyes,
musing on a kind of mind and imagination different from his own.

The clearest examples of this other kind of mind are Cathy and
Heathcliff. They both assume a spiritual reality beyond their merely
physical existence, and they need to believe in that reality as
desperately as Nelly and Lockwood need their empiricism:

"I cannot express it; but surely you and everybody have a notion that
there is, or should be an existence of yours beyond you. What were
the use of my creation if I were entirely contained here?" (Ch. IX)

This is Cathy, just before her declaration of "love" for Heathcliff
("Nelly, I *am* Heathcliff—he's always, always in my mind . . ."").
For her, there "is, or should be" some existence beyond the visible,
yet suggested by and known through it. Her feeling of relatedness to
Heathcliff is both source and confirmation of this other level of
existence.

Towards the end of the novel, as we are shown more of how
Heathcliff's mind works, we see that he too is clearly unable to see
"only" objects:

"Nelly, there is a strange change approaching—I'm in its shadow
at present—I take so little interest in my daily life, that I hardly

remember to eat and drink—Those two who have left the room are
the only objects which retain a distinct material appearance to
me. . . .

"Five minutes ago, Hareton seemed a personification of my youth,
not a human being—I felt to him in such a variety of ways, that it
would have been impossible to have accosted him rationally.

"In the first place, his startling likeness to Catherine connected
him fearfully with her—That however which you may suppose the
most potent to arrest my imagination, is actually the least—for
what is not connected with her to me? And what does not recall
her? . . . The entire world is a dreadful collection of memoranda
that she did exist, and that I have lost her!" (Ch. XXXIII)

Nelly observes, afterward, that this is another example of Heathcliff's "monomania," and that she considers him sound of wit in
every other respect. When he defines his state as being "half conscious," he means that he is approaching his true goal of full consciousness; for Nelly, he is moving *away* from full, or rational consciousness. The mingling of his dust with Cathy's, which he takes
steps to assure, is an example of the consciousness towards which he
is moving. In it the metaphorical association between physical as-
similation and spiritual union becomes a directly perceived cer-
tainty.

The latticed window, opening from the enclosed wooden bed, is
the most important focus for the problem of differing modes of
consciousness in the novel. Like life itself, this strange window may
open into another dimension. As children, Cathy and Heathcliff
shared the bed and enjoyed an impulsiveness and heightened awareness of the natural world. Rather than lose this sensibility they
rebel, against what Nelly is later to call "the sentiments of sober,
disenchanted maturity." The first glimpse we have of them is through
Cathy's eyes, on the brink of rebellion. Cathy's narrative ends with
her plans for a scamper on the moor in the rain, beneath the dairy
woman's cloak. It is not until Heathcliff's account of that night's
scamper that we learn the rebellion was abortive. Caught by the
Lintons' dog, she was taken inside the Grange and magically transformed into an adult. Heathcliff tries to follow her ("Nelly, make
me decent, I'm going to be good."), but is frustrated, and decides
instead to be bad. During his three-years' absence, he too is magically
changed into an adult. When he returns the sober tranquility of
the Grange ("still as death" and "wondrously peaceful") is shattered.
Cathy becomes "breathless and wild," with an abandoned "delight"
and "joy" discordant with the controls of sober maturity. The three
years' maturation has gone only skin deep. Cathy is torn between her

love for Edgar, with his considerate, paternal affection, and her love
for Heathcliff who offers a return to the unself-conscious intensity of
childlike emotions.

There is no possibility of resolution for her conflict, and in our
last full glimpse of her she lies looking out her bedroom window
at the Grange, her body in her grown-up bed, but her mind fixed
on the Heights and the past:

> "Nelly, I'll tell you what I thought, and what has kept recurring and
> recurring till I feared for my reason—I thought . . . that I was
> enclosed in the oak-panelled bed at home; and my heart ached with
> some great grief which, just waking, I could not recollect—I pondered,
> and worried myself to discover what it could be; and most strangely,
> the whole last seven years of my life grew a blank! I did not recall
> that they had been at all. I was a child; my father was just buried,
> and my misery arose from the separation that Hindley had ordered
> between me and Heathcliff—I was laid alone, for the first time. . . .
> I cannot say why I felt so wildly wretched . . . But, supposing at
> twelve years old, I had been wrenched from the Heights, and every
> early association, and my all in all, as Heathcliff was at that time,
> and been converted, at a stroke, into Mrs. Linton, the lady of Thrush-
> cross Grange, and the wife of a stranger, an exile, and outcast, thence-
> forth, from what had been my world—You may fancy a glimpse of
> the abyss where I grovelled! . . . I wish I were a girl again, half
> savage and hardy, and free . . . and laughing at injuries, not madden-
> ing under them! Why am I so changed?" (Ch. XII)

She can neither stay a girl, nor live separated from what had been
her world, and she dies.

The fact that it began in childhood does not necessarily debase
the relationship between Cathy and Heathcliff or their outlook on
life. Nor is it surprising that the only way of revealing either is
through dramatic mental regression and the metaphors of childhood.
Most of the Romantic poets (but especially Blake and Wordsworth) felt that they had to explore and understand the differences
between the joyfully innocent vision of the child, with its capacity
for unified experience, and the "sober, disenchanted" world of
the adult mind. The "abyss" which Cathy is trying to describe to
Nelly is the starting point of Wordsworth's "Intimations Ode,"
which charts the child's development from the "Heaven" of infancy,
with its "clouds of glory," to the death of this glory in "the light of
common day."

The window in the closet-bed suggests the existence of this earlier
world. Being in its presence and reading Cathy's marginalia have
strange effects on Lockwood, who is forced to break the window and

put his hand out to silence something that is disturbing him. When he does, he is terrified by the face and voice of a little girl, and the "tenacious gripe" of her hand. Reading the "faded hieroglyphics" of Cathy's "unformed, childish hand" (anticipating the "hand" at the window) has called up something from his own faded past, some long-repressed spirit of the child that he was, the child still in him that he thought dead. Cathy's description of her rebellion releases this spirit in him, and he fights it in the cruelest, most violent scene in the book:

> Terror made me cruel; and, finding it useless to attempt shaking the creature off, I pulled its wrist on to the broken pane, and rubbed it to and fro till the blood ran down and soaked the bedclothes: still it wailed, "Let me in!" and maintained its tenacious gripe, almost maddening me with fear. (Ch. III)

The true horror of this is that Lockwood is denying a part of himself, closing it out and piling up a pyramid of books between himself and the past.[3] In this scene at the window, we are shown what it means for Lockwood to be "locked" in from himself, locked into the rational, civilized part of himself that fears the other. He has chosen society's equivalent of "Th Helmet uh Salvation," because to do otherwise is to risk "T' Broad Way to Destruction." Beneath his suave control is the kind of fear that comes out in his dream of the famous Jabes Branderham's sermon—at the end, "Every man's hand was against his neighbor." The congregation has forgiven the required number of times, and can now release its destructive energies. Lockwood began the violence, urging an attack on Branderham ("Drag him down, and crush him to atoms . . ."). All this violence was suggested, according to Lockwood, "merely" by "the branch of a fir-tree that touched my lattice." This is as good a way as any for him to avoid learning that it is his own violence, his own potential for emotional experience that he fears.

The struggle that we see acted out in Chapter III lies behind Lockwood's first plea for our sympathy. In Chapter I, he describes how he first encouraged, then repulsed, the affections of a young girl:

> While enjoying a month of fine weather at the sea-coast, I was thrown into the company of a most fascinating creature. . . . if looks have language, the merest idiot might have guessed I was over head and

---

[3] There is a significant difference in the novel between books orderly arranged in the library, where both Edgar and Lockwood hide from experience, and books which are out, being used and thrown about.

ears; she understood me, at last, and looked a return—the sweetest
of all imaginable looks—and what did I do? I confess it with shame—
shrunk icily into myself, like a snail; at every glance retired colder and
farther; till, finally the poor innocent was led to doubt her own
senses, and overwhelmed with confusion at her supposed mistake,
persuaded her mamma to decamp.

We are supposed to feel sorry for Lockwood in this, and it is hard
not to. To use his own words, his "heartlessness" is not "deliberate."
He is an extreme but plausible example of civilized man, doing and
suffering violence to himself, partly from fatalism, partly from fear.

What Lockwood fears and resists is what Heathcliff and Cathy
have a remarkable ability to achieve. Heathcliff easily wrenches open
the lattice that stopped Lockwood, "bursting, as he pulled at it,
into an uncontrollable passion of tears." Simultaneous with the
opening of the window is the loss of what Lockwood calls "apparent sense," a surrender to passion which he finds embarrassing
to watch and beyond comprehension. Heathcliff's final surrender
to passion comes with his death. He dies before this same window—
the lattice open and the rain coming in, his hand on the sill—confident that his death will be the recovery of the happiness he had
glimpsed as a child. In this scene, as in the others, the window
suggests a threshold of vision and functions as a touchstone of
identity.

If we step back now, from contrasting these two contradictory ways
of seeing in the book, how can we determine which is the right
one? The implication behind such a question is that Emily Brontë
will have committed herself and the book to the verification of one
of the contrasting attitudes. If the reader identifies Nelly Dean as
the author's voice of reason, as the center and norm of vision for
the novel, then his experience of the story will be of one kind. On
the other hand, if he detects an ironic undercutting of Nelly and
Lockwood, their vision will not be trusted. The valid sensibilities
will then be Cathy's and Heathcliff's. What both extremes overlook
is the possibility that the novel is about the problem of contrasted
vision itself, perhaps even about the impossibility of adopting
decisively one or the other mode of vision. The difference here is
between reading the novel as "articulation," leading to fuller understanding of a problem's complexities, and reading it as the
"assertion" of an answer to the problem.

It is too easy, when discussing Heathcliff and the other characters
in the book, to end up with dehumanized images or symbols—to
turn Heathcliff into a mode of vision only, a natural force, a spirit of

rebellion, or sexual energy; to see Lockwood as a civilized puppet or narrative convenience, Nelly as a voice of reason, Joseph as a religious hypocrite. Their actions, as human beings, do have implications which can be followed in any of these directions. But to see only those implications which fit a particular formula is to do violence to the essentially human complexity of the characters, and to supply equations which Emily Brontë deliberately refrained from supplying.

There is no single meaning, no single system or theory of perceptions or values which the book points to and stands for. It does not allegorize Emily Brontë's private beliefs or theory of the world; yet what possibilities of belief, what doubts and fears she had, are in it, as are the whole range of possible explanations which we may call her "vision." The novel for us then is like the problem of life. We can solve it with any of a number of theories or systems, none of which fits perfectly. There is a narrowness in such interpretations when pushed too far, for her vision was basically one of infinite possibilities and few certainties. Keats has named this quality of vision "Negative Capability" (". . . that is when man is capable of being in uncertainties, mysteries, doubts, without any irritable reaching after fact and reason"). *Wuthering Heights* was written in this spirit; and the closer we come to reading it that way, the better readers we will be.

The Structure of *Wuthering Heights*

by Charles Percy Sanger

By common consent *Wuthering Heights* is a remarkable book. I do not propose to discuss its literary merits, but to confine myself to the humbler task of investigating its structure, which presents certain peculiarities. Whether this is worth doing I do not know, but I found that it added to my interest in the book and made the tale much more vivid for me.

The main theme is how a sort of human cuckoo, called Heathcliff, sets out with success to acquire all the property of two families, the Earnshaws and the Lintons. The tale is a fairly complicated one, and the incidents extend over a period of more than thirty years. Stated as baldly and shortly as I can, the plot is as follows: Mr. and Mrs. Earnshaw live at Wuthering Heights, a farm-house on a Yorkshire moor. They have two children, a son called Hindley and a daughter Catherine. One day Mr. Earnshaw, who has been to Liverpool on business, brings home a waif he has picked up there. This waif, Heathcliff, is brought up at Wuthering Heights. Not long after, Mrs. Earnshaw dies. Heathcliff is Mr. Earnshaw's favorite; he is also great friends with Catherine, but Hindley, who is older, bullies him. At last, Hindley is sent off to college. When Mr. Earnshaw dies, Hindley returns for the funeral, bringing with him a young wife. He takes possession, ill-treats Heathcliff, thrusts him into the position of a mere servant, and allows him no more education. But Catherine and Heathcliff have remained great friends, and one Sunday they go for a walk, and out of curiosity look at Thrushcross Grange, a gentleman's house in a park four miles off where Mr. and Mrs. Linton live. Catherine and Heathcliff peep in through the drawing-room window and see the two Linton children—Edgar

"*The Structure of* Wuthering Heights," *a paper originally read to the Heretics, a society at Cambridge University (London, Hogarth Press Ltd., 1926). Reprinted by permission of Miss Daphne Sanger and Chatto and Windus Ltd.*

and Isabella. The Lintons, hearing Heathcliff and Catherine and
taking them for robbers, let the bulldog loose on them; the dog
seizes Catherine and hurts her ankle badly. She is taken in and
looked after at Thrushcross Grange for five weeks, and returns to
Wuthering Heights elegantly dressed. Heathcliff, who is very dirty
and untidy, is ashamed. The next day the two Lintons come to
dinner; Heathcliff behaves ill and is punished by Hindley. The next
year Hindley's wife gives birth to a son—Hareton. She, however, is
consumptive and does not survive long. In despair at her death
Hindley takes to drink. When Catherine is fifteen Edgar Linton proposes to her. She accepts him, feeling all the time that she is doing
wrong because she loves Heathcliff. She tells Hareton's nurse, Ellen
Dean, about it; Heathcliff overhears part of the conversation, runs
off and vanishes. Catherine is distracted by this, gets fever, and when
convalescent goes to stay at Thrushcross Grange. Her host and
hostess, Mr. and Mrs. Linton, both catch the fever and die. This may
be considered the end of the first stage of the story. The elder generation are all dead. The next generation are all alive—Hindley and
Catherine at Wuthering Heights, Edgar and Isabella at Thrushcross Grange. Hindley's wife is dead, but his son Hareton—the only
representative of the third generation—is alive. Heathcliff has dis-
appeared. His passion for Catherine and his revenge is the main
theme of the root of the story.

Catherine in due course marries Edgar and goes to live at Thrushcross Grange. After six months of happiness, Heathcliff, who has
meanwhile mysteriously got some education and money, reappears.
He sets himself to ruin Hindley, who gambles and drinks. He also
finds that Isabella is in love with him, and decides to marry her to
get her money. One day, after a violent scene between Heathcliff
and Edgar, Catherine goes on hunger strike and gets brain fever.
Isabella elopes with Heathcliff, who treats her abominably, and
finally brings her back to Wuthering Heights. One Sunday while
Edgar is at church, Heathcliff comes to see Catherine. There is a
passionate scene. That night Catherine gives birth to a daughter and
dies. On the night after the funeral, Hindley tries to kill Heathcliff
but is nearly killed by him. Isabella escapes from Wuthering Heights
and goes to the South of England, where she gives birth to a sickly
child named Linton Heathcliff. Soon after this Hindley dies of drink,
and Heathcliff is left in possession of Wuthering Heights with Hareton, whom, out of revenge for the way he was treated as a boy, he
brings up as a mere brute. At this stage there is a long gap in the
story. Edgar's daughter, who is also called Catherine, lives with him

at Thrushcross Grange; Isabella's son, Linton, lives in the South
of England with her. Catherine is kept in ignorance of both her
cousins Linton and Hareton.

Edgar hears that Isabella is dying and goes to see her. Catherine
in his absence goes to Penistone Crags, and in doing so has to pass
Wuthering Heights, where she sees Hareton. On Isabella's death,
Edgar comes home with Linton, but Heathcliff claims him, and he
is taken to Wuthering Heights. Catherine is not allowed by Edgar,
her father, to go there. One day, after some time, Catherine on a
walk meets Heathcliff and Hareton and goes to Wuthering Heights,
where she sees her cousin, Linton. Catherine and Linton correspond
secretly. The correspondence is detected and stopped. Catherine's
father, Edgar, becomes ill. Heathcliff meets Catherine and tells her
that Linton is seriously ill. She goes to see him, and many times
visits him secretly. One day, just before her father dies, she is
kidnapped by Heathcliff and forced to marry Linton. Soon after
Linton dies, having made a will leaving all his personal property
to his father, Heathcliff. Heathcliff takes possession of Thrushcross
Grange, and lets it to Mr. Lockwood, who tells the story. But Heathcliff dies soon after, and Hareton and Catherine marry.

How is a long story like this to be told? How is the reader's interest to be excited? How is the tale to be kept together? How are
we to be made to feel the lapse of time without being pestered by
dates? How far did the authoress accurately visualize the ages of the
characters in the different incidents, the topography, and so on?
And how did Heathcliff succeed in getting the property? These are
the questions I attempt to answer.

The most obvious thing about the structure of the story which
deals with three generations is the symmetry of the pedigree. Mr.
and Mrs. Earnshaw at Wuthering Heights and Mr. and Mrs. Linton
at Thrushcross Grange each have one son and one daughter. Mr.
Linton's son marries Mr. Earnshaw's daughter, and their only child
Catherine marries successively her two cousins—Mr. Linton's grandson and Mr. Earnshaw's grandson. See the following pedigree: [p.
18].

In actual life I have never come across a pedigree of such absolute
symmetry. I shall have to refer to this pedigree again later. It is a
remarkable piece of symmetry in a tempestuous book.

The method adopted to arouse the reader's interest and to give
vividness and reality to the tale is one which has been used with
great success by Joseph Conrad. But it requires great skill.

After Edgar Linton's death, Mr. Lockwood, the narrator, takes

MR. EARNSHAW d. Oct. 1777.   *m.*   MRS. EARNSHAW d. Spring 1773.

MR. LINTON d. Autumn 1780.   *m.*   MRS. LINTON d. Autumn 1780.

HINDLEY b. Summer 1757. d. Sept. 1784.

Frances b. d. late 1778.

m. 1777.

CATHERINE b. Summer 1765. d. Mar. 20, 1784.

HARETON b. June 1778.

m. Jan. 1, 1803.

m. April 1783.

EDGAR b. 1762. d. Sept. 1801.

Heathcliff b. 1764. d. May 1802.

ISABELLA b. late 1765. d. June 1797.

m. Jan. 1784.

CATHERINE b. Mar. 20, 1784.

m. Aug. 1801.

LINTON b. Sept. 1784. d. Oct. 1801.

18

Thrushcross Grange for a year. He goes to call on his landlord, Heathcliff, at Wuthering Heights, and is puzzled to find there a *farouche* young woman and an awkward boor. At first he supposes Catherine to be Heathcliff's wife; when told she is his daughter-in-law, he then supposes that Hareton is Heathcliff's son, and has again to be corrected. He, and the reader, are naturally puzzled at this strange trio. Lockwood calls again, and is forced to spend the night because of a heavy fall of snow. In his room he finds some books with the name Catherine Earnshaw and Catherine Linton, and a sort of diary of Catherine's in a childish hand which gives a vivid picture of the situation just after her father's death. Mr. Lockwood has a nightmare in which Catherine's spirit comes to the window, and he also witnesses a strange scene of Heathcliff imploring Catherine's spirit. Our interest cannot fail now to be excited. What is this strange man and this strange menage? Who was this Catherine who died years before? What were her relations with Heathcliff? Naturally, Lockwood is much intrigued. On his way back next day he catches a chill and becomes ill. To pass the time he asks Ellen Dean, the housekeeper at Thrushcross Grange, what she knows about the family at Wuthering Heights. She, who was first Hareton's nurse and then the young Catherine's, tells him the story of the past thirty years in considerable detail. So that during the major part of the book Mr. Lockwood is telling us what Ellen Dean told him, but sometimes, also, what Ellen Dean told him that someone else—for instance, Isabella—had told her. Only a small part, perhaps one-tenth of the book, consists of direct narrative by Lockwood from his own knowledge. But such a scheme may be confusing, and it is easy to muddle the time. Did Emily Brontë realize and let us know the dates when each event happened? She did, but not by giving them directly. Look again at the pedigree. The dates there have all been derived from the book, yet only one is directly stated. What first brought me to study the book more closely was when I noticed that the first word in the book was a date—1801. I thought this must have some significance. Similarly, the first word of Chapter XXXII is 1802. Apart from this, only one other date is given directly. In the last sentence of Chapter VII, Ellen Dean says, "I will be content to pass on to the next summer—the summer of 1778, that is, nearly twenty-three years ago." This gives no further information, as 1801 is twenty-three years after 1778, but in the first sentence of the next chapter she tells us that Hareton was born in June. This is how I get June 1778 for Hareton's birth in the pedigree. But what about the rest of the dates, not only those in the pedigree but of all the

incidents in the story? There are a considerable number (perhaps
nearly a hundred) indications of various kinds to help us—intervals
of time, ages of characters, the months, the harvest moon, the last
grouse, and so forth, and we learn, incidentally, that the younger
Catherine's birthday was on 20th March. Sometimes, too, we know
the day of the week—thus Ellen Dean will remember something
which happened on a Sunday, or on a Christmas Eve. Taking all
these indications, it is, I think, possible to ascertain the year, and, in
most cases, the month of the year in which every event takes place
—also the ages of the various characters, except, naturally, there is
a slight doubt as to Heathcliff, because no one knows his exact age
when he was found by Mr. Earnshaw. But one has to go warily and
consider all the indications together, for there is a curious subtlety
that sometimes the characters are described as *looking* some ages
which are not exact. Thus Lockwood when he first describes them
says that Heathcliff was about forty and Catherine did not look
seventeen. In fact, Catherine was seventeen and three-quarters and
Heathcliff cannot have been more than thirty-eight. It would be
too tedious to state the process by which I have discovered each
date (see Appendix). But I will give one or two illustrations. We
already know that Hareton was born in June 1778; we are told
that he was nearly five when Catherine Earnshaw married Edgar
Linton, so that the marriage was before June 1783. But Heathcliff
returned in September after they had been happily married for six
months. Thus the marriage was in April 1783. We are told that the
scene that led to Catherine's death was a Sunday in the March
after Heathcliff's return, and that her daughter, Catherine, was born
about midnight, and the mother died two hours after. Later on we
learn that Catherine's birthday was the 20th (and that this was also
treated as the day of her mother's death). Hence Catherine died at
2 A.M. on Monday, 20th March 1784.

I will give only one other instance. Lockwood begins his account
in 1801; it is snowy weather, which might be in January or February
or in November or December. But he returns in 1802 before his
year's tenancy is out. Hence the story begins at the end of 1801. A
Michaelmas tenancy begins at the 10th October—not on 29th
September—because when the calendar was reformed eleven days
were left out. Therefore, the story begins after 10th October 1801.
Now after Lockwood has been ill three weeks Heathcliff sends him
some grouse, the last of the season. Since the Game Act, 1831, grouse
may not be shot after 10th December, so we may take this as about
the date for the last grouse. Thus the story begins about the middle

of November, and this fits pretty well with the later indications. That
is sufficient to illustrate the process. Sometimes it is only by fitting
together several indications, each rather vague, that one can find the
month. There is, however, one curious fact. We can ascertain
Hindley's age. Now Ellen Dean was of the same age. She was his
foster sister, and the doctor also refers to her as being of the same
age as Hindley. Yet she makes two mistakes about her own age.
Middle-aged people do, of course, make mistakes about their age,
and these slips may have been intentional on the part of Emily
Brontë, but, if so, it seems to me a little over-subtle.

The topography is equally precise. On going from Thrushcross
Grange to the village of Gimmerton a highway branches off to the
moor on the left. There is a stone pillar there. Thrushcross Grange
lies to the south-west, Gimmerton to the east, and Wuthering Heights
to the north. The distance from Thrushcross Grange to Wuthering
Heights is four miles, and Penistone Crags lie a mile and a half
farther on. It was half an hour from Gimmerton to Thrushcross
Grange.

The botany is sure to be correct. Emily Brontë loved the country.
I was a little surprised to find an ash tree in bud as early as 20th
March, but then I realized that it was not on the moor but in the
park at Thrushcross Grange, which lay low and was no doubt
sheltered.

I now come to the final problem. Heathcliff schemed to get all
the property of both the Earnshaws and the Lintons. How did he
do it? Emily Brontë clearly had a considerable knowledge of the
law. We know the source of George Eliot's use of a base fee for the
plot of Felix Holt. We do not know the source of Jane Austen's
unerring grasp of the law of real property; but she lived among
people who had settled estates and could easily have obtained it. But
how Emily Brontë acquired her knowledge I cannot guess. There
is also this difficulty. *Wuthering Heights* was written in the eighteen-
forties. It was published in 1847. But the period of the tale is from
1771 to 1803. The Inheritance Act of 1834, the Wills Act of 1837,
and, I think, the Game Act of 1831, had changed the law. Did Emily
Brontë apply the law at the time she wrote or that at the period of
the tale? In one case, as we shall see, she used the earlier law.

Novelists sometimes make their plots depend on the law and use
legal terms. But they frequently make mistakes and sometimes are
absurd as Trollope is in *Orley Farm*. What is remarkable about
Wuthering Heights is that the ten or twelve legal references are, I
think, sufficient to enable us to ascertain the various legal processes

by which Heathcliff obtained the property. It is not a simple matter.
There was a fundamental difference between the law of land (real
property) and that of money and goods (personal property).

Let us begin with Wuthering Heights. The Earnshaws were
farmers and not likely to have their estate settled. The property
had been in their family since 1500. We may take it then that Mr.
Earnshaw was owner in fee-simple, that is in effect absolute owner,
of Wuthering Heights, and was not likely to have possessed any
investments. It is more likely that there was a mortgage on the house
and farm. On Mr. Earnshaw's death the land descended to Hindley
as his heir-at-law. There is no mention of a will. The personal property, which, probably, was only the farming stock and the furniture,
would go equally to his children, Hindley and Catherine, subject to
the payment of his debts out of it. On Catherine's marriage Edgar
would have become entitled to her personal property. Now Hindley
drinks and gambles away all he has, and at his death the property
is mortgaged up to the hilt. Heathcliff we find is the mortgagee. The
personal property would also be liable to the debts. So that Heathcliff is mortgagee in possession and, for practical purposes, owner
of all the Earnshaw property except any personalty that had gone
to Catherine. This is all fairly simple; but it is more difficult when
we come to the Linton property. They were landed gentry; they had
a park, they had tenants. Mr. Linton, and Edgar after him, was a
magistrate. Such people, generally, had a settlement of their land,
and we find, in fact, that Mr. Linton had settled it by his will. To
understand what happens it is necessary to go into the intricacies of
real property law and to look at the pedigree.

I must explain very shortly the law of entails. What is called an
estate tail is an estate which descends according to the following
rules: (1) Males are preferred to females; (2) males take in order
according to seniority of birth, but females take equally; (3) descendants represent their ancestor. In case of a conflict between
them, rule (3) prevails. A tenant in tail of full age in possession
could by means of a fictitious action (for which a deed was sub-
stituted by the Fines and Recoveries Act, 1833) bar the entail and
obtain the fee-simple, which practically amounts to absolute owner-
ship. By his will a testator could settle his land on living persons
for life, but could not give life estates to the children of such persons
who were not alive at the testator's death. Consequently, if he
wanted to tie up his estate as long as possible, he gave life estates
to such of his descendants as were living at his death, followed by
estates tail to their children.

Now the settlement made by Mr. Linton's will must have been as follows: The estate was devised to Edgar, his only son, for life, then to Edgar's sons in tail; Edgar's daughters were passed over in favor of Mr. Linton's daughter, Isabella, who, presumably, had a life interest with remainder to her sons in tail. This is the usual form. Thus on Edgar Linton's death, Linton Heathcliff became tenant in tail in possession during the few weeks he survived his uncle. As a minor he could not bar the entail. It is most improbable that he had an estate in fee-simple; that would have been too unusual. Isabella might have had an estate tail instead of a life interest. This is most improbable, but if she did, her son, Linton Heathcliff, would have become tenant in tail by descent, so the result is the same. Heathcliff claims the property—by what right? Ellen Dean says that he claimed and kept the Thrushcross Grange estate in his wife's right and in his son's also. She adds: "I suppose, legally at any rate, Catherine, destitute of cash and friends, cannot disturb his possession." She is quite right in her suspicions. Even if Isabella had had an estate tail, or even an estate in fee-simple, Heathcliff would not have had any right as husband to an estate for life—the estate known as an estate by courtesy—because Isabella was never in possession. And even if, which to my mind is not possible, Linton Heathcliff had had an estate in fee-simple, his father would not have been his heir before the Inheritance Act, 1833, because it was considered unnatural that an inheritance should ascend directly; and, as Ellen Dean knows and states, Linton Heathcliff as a minor could not dispose of his land by will. There is no difficulty as to the personal property. Whatever Isabella had Heathcliff got by marrying her. There was no Married Women's Property Act in these days. They eloped, so there was no question of a marriage settlement. Edgar Linton had saved out of his rents to make a provision for his daughter, Catherine. When dying he decides, in order to prevent Heathcliff getting at them, to alter his will so as to settle them on Catherine for life and then for her children. The attorney for whom he sends is, however, kept from going by Heathcliff, and Edgar dies before his will is altered, so the money passes to Catherine and then to her husband, Linton. He, though a minor, could (before the year 1838) make a will of personalty. He is induced or forced to do so, and leaves it all to Heathcliff.

Thus, at Heathcliff's death, the position seems to be that he has acquired all the personal property of both families: he is mortgagee in possession of Wuthering Heights, and is, though wrongfully, in possession of Thrushcross Grange, which he has let to Lockwood.

He thinks of making a will but does not do so. What then happens on his death? He has no relations, so that his real property will escheat, and his personal property will go to the Crown as *bona vacantia*. What then becomes of Hareton and Catherine who, when the tale ends, are to be happily married on New Year's Day, 1803? At one time I thought this was the climax of the tragedy. These young people, ill-educated and incompetent, were to be left destitute. But that would be going too far. Catherine, as you will see from the pedigree, is the sole living descendant of Mr. Linton. In some way or other, I need not go through the various alternatives, she must have become entitled to Thrushcross Grange, which is plainly by far the most valuable property. Heathcliff had been mortgagee in possession of Wuthering Heights for eighteen years, but this was not long enough to obtain an absolute title by adverse possession. Hareton, as Hindley's heir, would be entitled to the equity of redemption. Now if Heathcliff, who managed well, properly accounted for his profits during the eighteen years as he could be made to do, it may well be that they were sufficient, if he was charged a proper occupation rent, to pay off the mortgage. So that Hareton would get the house and land unencumbered or, at any rate, only slightly burdened. The personal property was comparatively unimportant, and we can only hope that the Crown did not insist on its rights, if it knew of them, or that if it did insist, the happy couple could buy out the Crown's claim out of the rent which Lockwood, as we know, paid.

There is, so far as I know, no other novel in the world which it is possible to subject to an analysis of the kind I have tried to make. This in itself makes the book very unusual. Did the authoress carry all the dates in her head, or did she work with a calendar? Was 20th March 1784, for example, on a Monday? According to my calculations it was not, it was a Saturday, but I should like to have this confirmed by some competent chronologist; for if I am right, it shows that Emily Brontë did not use a calendar, and that nothing will be gained by finding out, for instance, the date of Easter in 1803.

However dull and technical the above details may be, they do, I believe, throw a light on the character of Emily Brontë and her book. German romances can hardly have been the source of her knowledge of English law. A great critic has spoken of the passionate chastity of the book; but the extreme care in realizing the ages of the characters at the time of each incident which is described seems to

me a more unusual characteristic of a novel. It demonstrates the
vividness of the author's imagination.

Appendix: Chronology of Wuthering Heights

CHAP.			
	1757,	before September.	Hindley Earnshaw born.
	1762,	"	Edgar Linton born.
	1764,	"	Heathcliff born.
	1765,	summer.	Catherine Earnshaw born.
	"	late.	Isabella Linton born.
IV.	1771,	summer, beginning of harvest.	Heathcliff brought to Wuthering Heights.
	1773,	spring or early summer.	Mrs. Earnshaw dies.
V.	1774,	October.	Hindley sent to college.
	1777,		Hindley marries.
	"		Mr. Earnshaw dies.
VI.	"		Hindley returns with his wife.
III.	"	October or November.	The scene described by Catherine.
VI.	"	November, third week, Sunday.	Catherine and Heathcliff go to Thrushcross Grange.
VII.	"	Christmas Eve.	Catherine returns to W. H.
	"	Christmas Day.	The Lintons visit W. H.
VIII.	1778,	June.	Hareton Earnshaw born.
	"	late.	Frances Earnshaw dies.
	1780,	summer.	Edgar Linton calls at W. H. and proposes to Catherine.
IV.	"	"	Hindley returns drunk.
	"	"	Catherine tells Ellen about Edgar.
	"	"	Heathcliff goes off.
IV.	1780,	summer.	Catherine gets wet through and catches fever.
	"	autumn.	Catherine, convalescent, goes to Thrushcross Grange. Mr. and Mrs. Linton catch the fever and die.
	1783,	April.	Edgar marries Catherine.
X.	"	September.	Heathcliff returns and sees Catherine.
	"	autumn.	Isabella falls in love with Heathcliff, who visits Thrushcross Grange from time to time.

CHAP.

XI.	1783,	December.	Ellen Dean sees Hareton.
			Heathcliff kisses Isabella.
	1784,	January 6, Monday.	Violent scene at Thrushcross Grange. Heathcliff is turned out and Catherine goes on hunger strike.
XII.	"	January 10, Friday.	Catherine delirious.
	"	" " 2 a.m.	Isabella elopes with Heathcliff.
XIII.	"	March 13, Monday.	The Heathcliffs return to W. H.
XIV.	"	March 15, Wednes-day.	Ellen Dean goes to W. H.
XV.	"	March 19, Sunday.	Heathcliff sees Catherine: violent scene.
XVI.	"	" midnight.	Catherine Linton born.
	"	March 20, Monday, 2 a.m.	Catherine (the elder) dies.
	"	March 21, Tuesday.	Heathcliff puts a lock of hair in Catherine's locket.
	"	March 24, Friday.	Catherine's funeral.
XVII.	"	same day, midnight.	Heathcliff nearly kills Hindley, who tried to kill him.
	"	March 25, Satur-day.	Isabella runs off.
XVII.	1784,	September.	Linton Heathcliff born.
	"	September or Oc-tober.	Hindley Earnshaw dies. All his property is mortgaged to Heathcliff.
XVIII.	1797,	early June.	Catherine goes to Penistone Crags and meets Hareton.
XIX.	"	June.	Isabella dies. Edgar brings back Linton Heathcliff.
XX.	"	"	Linton Heathcliff is taken to live at Wuthering Heights.
XXI.	1800,	March 20.	Catherine and Ellen meet Hareton, and go to Wuthering Heights where they see Linton.
	"	March or April.	Catherine and Linton corre-spond.
XXII.	"	late October or November.	Catherine sees Heathcliff, who says that Linton is seriously ill.
XXIII.	"	late October or November.	Catherine and Ellen go to see Linton. Ellen catches cold and is ill for three weeks.
XXIV.	"	November.	During Ellen's illness Catherine visits Linton secretly.

CHAP.

XXV.	1801,	March 20.	Edgar too ill to visit his wife's grave.
	"	June.	Edgar declining.
XXVI.	"	August.	Ellen and Catherine go to meet Linton.
	"	August, Thursday, a week later	They are kidnapped.
	"	Monday?	Catherine and Linton marry.
XXVII.	"	August or September.	Ellen is let out.
	"	next Tuesday.	Edgar is dying; he sends for Mr. Green, the lawyer, who does not come.
XXVIII.	1801,	Wednesday, 3 a.m., harvest moon.	Catherine escapes and comes to Thrushcross Grange. Edgar Linton dies.
XXIX.	"	September, evening after the funeral.	Heathcliff comes to Wuthering Heights and takes off Catherine.
XXX.	"	October.	Linton Heathcliff dies. Hareton tries to please Catherine.
I.	"	late November.	Lockwood calls at W. H.
II.	"	next day.	He calls again and has to stay the night. He finds Catherine's diary and sees Heathcliff's outburst.
	"	next day.	Leaves at eight. Catches cold.
IV.	"	"	Ellen Dean begins her story.
X.	"	three weeks later.	Heathcliff sends grouse.
	"	one week later.	Heathcliff calls.
XV.	1802,	January, one week later.	Lockwood continues his account.
XXXI.	"	January, 2nd week.	Lockwood calls at W. H.
XXXII.	"	beginning of February.	Ellen goes to live at W. H.
	"	March.	Hareton has an accident.
	"	Easter Monday.	Catherine is nice to Hareton.
XXXIII.	"	Easter Tuesday.	Scene about altering garden.
	"	(after March 18.)	Heathcliff getting odd.
XXXIV.	"	April.	Heathcliff goes on hunger strike.
	"	May.	Heathcliff dies.
	"	September.	Lockwood visits Thrushcross Grange and Wuthering Heights.
XXXIV.	1803,	January 1.	Catherine and Hareton marry.

Emily Brontë: *Wuthering Heights*

by *Arnold Kettle*

Wuthering Heights, like all the greatest works of art, is at once concrete and yet general, local and yet universal. Because so much nonsense has been written and spoken about the Brontës and because Emily in particular has been so often presented to us as a ghost-like figure surrounded entirely by endless moorland, cut off from anything so banal as human society, not of her time but of eternity, it is necessary to emphasize at the outset the local quality of the book.

Wuthering Heights is about England in 1847. The people it reveals live not in a never-never land but in Yorkshire. Heathcliff was born not in the pages of Byron, but in a Liverpool slum. The language of Nelly, Joseph and Hareton is the language of Yorkshire people. The story of *Wuthering Heights* is concerned not with love in the abstract but with the passions of living people, with property-ownership, the attraction of social comforts, the arrangement of marriages, the importance of education, the validity of religion, the relations of rich and poor.

There is nothing vague about this novel; the mists in it are the mists of the Yorkshire moors; if we speak of it as having an elemental quality it is because the very elements, the great forces of nature are evoked, which change so slowly that in the span of a human life they seem unchanging. But in this evocation there is nothing sloppy or uncontrolled. On the contrary the realization is intensely concrete: we seem to smell the kitchen of Wuthering Heights, to feel the force of the wind across the moors, to sense the very changes of the seasons. Such concreteness is achieved not by mistiness but by precision.

It is necessary to stress this point but not, of course, to force it to

"Emily Brontë: Wuthering Heights," *from* An Introduction to the English Novel *(London, Hutchinson & Co. Ltd., 1951), Volume I, Part III. Reprinted by permission of Hutchinson & Co. Ltd.*

a false conclusion. The power and wonder of Emily Brontë's novel does not lie in naturalistic description, nor in a detailed analysis of the hour-by-hour issues of social living. Her approach is, quite obviously, not the approach of Jane Austen; it is much nearer to the approach of Dickens. Indeed, *Wuthering Heights* is essentially the same kind of novel as *Oliver Twist*. It is not a romance, not (despite the film bearing the same title) an escape from life to the wild moors and romantic lovers. It is certainly not a picaresque novel and it cannot adequately be described as a moral fable, though it has a strong, insistent pattern. But the pattern, like that of Dickens's novel, cannot be abstracted as a neat sentence: its germ is not an intellectualized idea or concept.

Emily Brontë works not in ideas but in symbols, that is to say concepts which have a significance and validity on a level different from that of logical thought. Just as the significance of the workhouse in *Oliver Twist* cannot adequately be conceived in merely logical terms but depends on a host of associations—including its physical shape and color—which logical analysis may penetrate but is unlikely adequately to convey, so the significance of the moors in *Wuthering Heights* cannot be suggested in the cold words of logic (which does not mean that it is illogical). The symbolic novel is an advance on the moral fable just in the sense that a symbol can be richer—can touch on more of life—than an abstract moral concept.

The opening sentence of the *Social Contract* gives a simple example: "Man was born free, but everywhere he is in chains." Of the two statements in this sentence the first is abstract, the second symbolic. And the impact of the second on our imagination is greater than that of the first for this very reason. (If one were concerned to go deeper into the matter one might suggest that Rousseau *knew* that man was in chains but merely speculated that he had been born free.) Now, whereas the symbolism of the moral fable (and the fable is itself a kind of extended symbol) is inherently limited by the abstract concept behind it, the symbolism of *Wuthering Heights* or the good part of *Oliver Twist* is the expression of the very terms in which the novel has been conceived.[1] In fact, it *is*

---

[1] A simple, though not infallible, indication of the kind of novel one is dealing with is given by the naming of characters. In allegory and the novel of 'humours' names always denote character—e.g., Faithful and Squire Allworthy. In totally non-symbolic novelists like Jane Austen the names are quite without significance: Emma Woodhouse might equally well be called Anne Elliot. In novels which have a certain symbolic quality the names of characters generally have a peculiar rightness of their own: Heathcliff, Noah Claypole, Henry James's characters.

the novel and the novel stands or falls by its validity, its total
adequacy to life.

Wuthering Heights is a vision of what life in 1847 was like.
Whether it can be described as a vision of what life as such—all life
—is like is a question we will consider later. It is, for all its appearance of casualness and the complexity of its family relationships, a very well-constructed book, in which the technical problems
of presentation have been most carefully thought out. The roles of
the two narrators, Lockwood and Nelly Dean, are not casual. Their
function (they the two most 'normal' people in the book) is partly
to keep the story close to the earth, to make it believable, partly to
comment on it from a common-sense point of view and thereby to
reveal in part the inadequacy of such common sense. They act as
a kind of sieve to the story, sometimes a double sieve, which has the
purpose not simply of separating off the chaff, but of making us
aware of the difficulty of passing easy judgments. One is left always
with the sense that the last word has not been said.

The narrators do not as a rule talk realistically, though sometimes Nelly's part is to slip into a Yorkshire dialect that 'places' what
she is describing and counteracts any tendency (inherent in symbolic
art) to the pretentious. At critical points in the narrative we are
not conscious of their existence at all; there is no attempt at a limit-
ing verisimilitude of speech. They do not impose themselves between us and the scene. But at other times their attitudes are important.

One of the subtleties of the book is the way these attitudes change
and develop; Lockwood and Nelly, like us, learn from what they
experience, though at first their limitations are made use of, as in the
very first scene when the expectations of the conventional Lockwood are so completely shocked by what he finds at Wuthering
Heights. He goes there, he the normal Victorian gentleman, expecting to find the normal Victorian middle-class family. And what
he finds—a house seething with hatred, conflict, horror—is a shock
to us, too. The attack on our complacency, moral, social and spiritual, has already begun.

The center and core of the book is the story of Catherine and
Heathcliff. It is a story which has four stages. The first part, ending
in the visit to Thrushcross Grange, tells of the establishing of a
special relationship between Catherine and Heathcliff and of their
common rebellion against Hindley and his regime in Wuthering
Heights. In the second part is revealed Catherine's betrayal of
Heathcliff, culminating in her death. The third part deals with

Heathcliff's revenge, and the final section, shorter than the others, tells of the change that comes over Heathcliff and of his death. Even in the last two sections, after her death, the relationship with Catherine remains the dominant theme, underlying all else that occurs.

It is not easy to suggest with any precision the quality of feeling that binds Catherine and Heathcliff. It is not primarily a sexual relationship. Emily Brontë is not, as is sometimes suggested, afraid of sexual love; the scene at Catherine's death is proof enough that this is no platonic passion, yet to describe the attraction as sexual is surely quite inadequate. Catherine tries to express her feelings to Nelly (she is about to marry Linton):

> "My great miseries in this world have been Heathcliff's miseries, and I watched and felt each from the beginning: my great thought in living is himself. If all else perished, and *he* remained, *I* should still continue to be; and if all else remained, and he were annihilated, the universe would turn to a mighty stranger: I should not seem a part of it. My love for Linton is like the foliage in the woods: time will change it, I'm well aware, as winter changes the trees. My love for Heathcliff resembles the eternal rocks beneath: a source of little visible delight, but necessary. Nelly, I *am* Heathcliff! He's always, always, in my mind: not as a pleasure, any more than I am always a pleasure to myself, but as my own being." [2]

and Heathcliff cries, when Catherine is dying: "I *cannot* live without my life, I *cannot* live without my soul." [3] What is conveyed to us here is the sense of an affinity deeper than sexual attraction, something which it is not enough to describe as romantic love.

This affinity is forged in rebellion and, in order to grasp the concrete and unromantic nature of this book, it is necessary to recall the nature of that rebellion. Heathcliff, the waif from the Liverpool slums, is treated kindly by old Mr. Earnshaw but insulted and degraded by Hindley. After his father's death Hindley reduces the boy to the status of a serf. "He drove him from their company to the servants, deprived him of the instructions of the curate, and insisted that he should labour out of doors instead; compelling him to do so as hard as any other hand on the farm." [4] The situation at Wuthering Heights is wonderfully evoked in the passage from Catherine's journal, which Lockwood finds in his bedroom:

[2] *Wuthering Heights,* Chap. IX.
[3] *Ibid.,* Chap. XVI.
[4] *Ibid.,* Chap. VI.

"An awful Sunday!" commenced the paragraph beneath. "I wish my father were back again. Hindley is a detestable substitute—his conduct to Heathcliff is atrocious—H. and I are going to rebel—we took our initiatory step this evening.

"All day had been flooding with rain; we could not go to church, so Joseph must needs get up a congregation in the garret, and, while Hindley and his wife basked downstairs before a comfortable fire— doing anything but reading the Bibles, I'll answer for it—Heathcliff, myself, and the unhappy plough-boy, were commanded to take our Prayer-books, and mount: were ranged in a row, on a sack of corn, groaning and shivering, and hoping that Joseph would shiver too, so that he might give us a short homily for his own sake. A vain idea! The service lasted precisely three hours: and yet my brother had the face to exclaim, when he saw us descending, 'What, done already?' On Sunday evenings we used to be permitted to play, if we did not make much noise; now a mere titter is sufficient to send us into corners!

" 'You forget you have a master here,' says the tyrant. 'I'll demolish the first who puts me out of temper! I insist on perfect sobriety and silence. Oh, boy! was that you? Frances darling, pull his hair as you go by: I heard him snap his fingers.' Frances pulled his hair heartily, and then went and seated herself on her husband's knee: and there they were, like two babies, kissing and talking nonsense by the hour —foolish palaver that we should be ashamed of. We made ourselves as snug as our means allowed in the arch of the dresser. I had just fastened our pinafores together, and hung them up for a curtain, when in comes Joseph on an errand from the stables. He tears down my handiwork boxes my ears and croaks—

" 'T' maister nobbut just buried, and Sabbath no o'ered, and t'sound o' t' gospel still i' yer lugs, and ye darr be laiking! Shame on ye! Sit ye down, ill childer! There's good books enough if ye'll read em! sit ye down, and think of yer sowls!'

"Saying this, he compelled us so to square our positions that we might receive from the far-off fire a dull ray to show us the text of the lumber he thrust upon us. I could not bear the employment. I took my dingy volume by the scroop, and hurled it into the dog-kennel, vowing I hated a good book. Heathcliff kicked his to the same place. Then there was a hubbub!

" 'Maister Hindley!' shouted our chaplain. 'Maister, coom hither! Miss Cathy's riven th' back of 'Th' Helmet O' Salvation,' un Heathcliff's pawsed his fit into t' first part o' 'T' Brooad Way to Destruction.' It's fair flaysome, that ye let 'em go on this gait. Ech! th' owd man wad ha' laced 'em properly—but he's goan!'

"Hindley hurried up from his paradise on the hearth, and seizing one of us by the collar, and the other by the arm, hurled both into the back kitchen, where, Joseph asseverated, 'owd Nick' would

fetch us as sure as we were living, and, so comforted, we each sought
a separate nook to await his advent." [5]

This passage reveals, in itself, a great deal of the extraordinary
quality of *Wuthering Heights*. It is a passage which, in the typical
manner of the novel, evokes, in language which involves the kind
of attention we give to poetry, a world far larger than the scene it
describes, and evokes it through the very force and concreteness
of the particular scene. The rebellion of Catherine and Heathcliff
is made completely concrete. They are not vague romantic dreamers.
Their rebellion is against the régime in which Hindley and his wife
sit in fatuous comfort by the fire whilst they are relegated to the
arch of the dresser and compelled for the good of their souls to
read the *Broad Way to Destruction* under the tutelage of the canting
hypocrite Joseph. It is a situation not confined, in the year 1847, to
the more distant homesteads of the Yorkshire moors.

Against this degradation Catherine and Heathcliff rebel, hurling
their pious books into the dog-kennel. And in their revolt they discover their deep and passionate need of each other. He, the outcast
slummy, turns to the lively, spirited, fearless girl who alone offers
him human understanding and comradeship. And she, born into the
world of Wuthering Heights, senses that to achieve a full humanity,
to be true to herself as a human being, she must associate herself
totally with him in his rebellion against the tyranny of the Earnshaws
and all that tyranny involves.

It is this rebellion that immediately, in this early section of the
book, wins over our sympathy to Heathcliff. We know he is on the
side of humanity and we are with him just as we are with Oliver
Twist, and for much the same reasons. But whereas Oliver is presented with a sentimental passivity, which limits our concern, Heathcliff is active and intelligent and able to carry the positive values of
human aspiration on his shoulders. He is a conscious rebel. And it is
from his association in rebellion with Catherine that the particular
quality of their relationship arises. It is the reason why each feels that
a betrayal of what binds them together is in some obscure and
mysterious way a betrayal of everything, of all that is most valuable
in life and death.

Yet Catherine betrays Heathcliff and marries Edgar Linton,
kidding herself that she can keep them both, and then discovering
that in denying Heathcliff she has chosen death. The conflict here
is, quite explicitly, a social one. Thrushcross Grange, embodying

[5] *Ibid.*, Chap. III.

as it does the prettier, more comfortable side of bourgeois life, seduces Catherine. She begins to despise Heathcliff's lack of 'culture.' He has no conversation, he does not brush his hair, he is dirty, whereas Edgar, besides being handsome, "will be rich and I shall like to be the greatest woman of the neighbourhood, and I shall be proud of having such a husband." [6] And so Heathcliff runs away and Catherine becomes mistress of Thrushcross Grange.

Heathcliff returns, adult and prosperous, and at once the social conflict is re-emphasized. Edgar, understandably, does not want to receive Heathcliff, but Catherine is insistent:

> "I know you didn't like him," she answered, repressing a little the intensity of her delight. "Yet, for my sake, you must be friends now. Shall I tell him to come up?"
>
> "Here," he said, "into the parlour?"
>
> "Where else?" she asked.
>
> He looked vexed, and suggested the kitchen as a more suitable place for him. Mrs. Linton eyed him with a droll expression—half angry, half laughing at his fastidiousness.
>
> "No," she added after a while; "I cannot sit in the kitchen. Set two tables here, Ellen: one for your master and Miss Isabella, being gentry, the other for Heathcliff and myself, being the lower orders. Will that please you, dear? . . ." [7]

And from the moment of Heathcliff's reappearance Catherine's attempts to reconcile herself to Thrushcross Grange are doomed. In their relationship now there is no tenderness, they trample on each other's nerves, madly try to destroy each other; but, once Heathcliff is near, Catherine can maintain no illusions about the Lintons. The two are united only in their contempt for the values of Thrushcross Grange. "There it is," Catherine taunts Edgar, speaking of her grave, "not among the Lintons, mind, under the chapel roof, but in the open air, with a headstone." [8] The open air, nature, the moors are contrasted with the world of Thrushcross Grange. And the contempt for the Lintons is a *moral* contempt, not a jealous one. When Nelly tells Heathcliff that Catherine is going mad, his comment is:

> "You talk of her mind being unsettled. How the devil could it be otherwise in her frightful isolation? And that insipid paltry creature attending her from *duty* and *humanity!* From *pity* and

charity! He might as well plant an oak in a flower pot, and expect it to thrive, as imagine he can restore her to vigour in the soil of his shallow cares!" [9]

The moral passion here is so intense, so deeply imbedded in the rhythm and imagery of the prose, that it is easy to be swept along without grasping its full and extraordinary significance. Heathcliff at this point has just perpetrated the first of his callous and ghastly acts of revenge, his marriage to Isabella. It is an act so morally repulsive that it is almost inconceivable that we should be able now to take seriously his attack on Edgar Linton, who has, after all, by conventional, respectable standards, done nobody any harm. And yet we *do* take the attack seriously because Emily Brontë makes us. The passion of the passage just quoted has the quality of great poetry. Why?

We continue to sympathize with Heathcliff, even after his marriage with Isabella, because Emily Brontë convinces us that what Heathcliff stands for is morally superior to what the Lintons stand for. This is, it must be insisted, not a case of some mysterious 'emotional' power with which Heathcliff is charged. The emotion behind his denunciation of Edgar is *moral* emotion. The words "duty" and "humanity," "pity" and "charity" have precisely the kind of force Blake gives such words in his poetry.[10]

They are used not so much paradoxically as in a sense inverted but more profound than the conventional usage. Heathcliff speaks, apparently paradoxically, of Catherine's "frightful isolation," when to all appearances she is in Thrushcross Grange less isolated, more subject to care and society, than she could possibly be with him. But in truth Heathcliff's assertion is a paradox only to those who do not understand his meaning. What he is asserting with such intense emotional conviction that we, too, are convinced, is that what he stands for, the alternative life *he* has offered Catherine is more natural (the image of the oak enforces this), more social and more moral than the world of Thrushcross Grange. Most of those who criticize Heathcliff adversely (on the grounds that he is unbelievable,

---

[9] *Ibid.,* Chap. XIV.
[10] E.g. Pity would be no more
     If we did not make somebody Poor;
     And Mercy no more could be
     If all were as happy as we

   or

     Was Jesus humble? or did he
     Give any proofs of Humility.

or that he is a neurotic creation, or that he is merely the Byronic satan-hero revived) fail to appreciate his significance because they fail to recognize this moral force. And as a rule they fail to recognize the moral force because they are themselves, consciously or not, of the Linton party.

The climax of this inversion by Heathcliff and Catherine of the common standards of bourgeois morality comes at the death of Catherine. To recognize the revolutionary force of this scene one has only to imagine what a different novelist might have made of it.

The stage is all set for a moment of conventional drama. Catherine is dying, Heathcliff appears out of the night. Two possibilities present themselves: either Catherine will at the last reject Heathcliff, the marriage vow will be vindicated and wickedness meet its reward; or true love will triumph and reconciliation proclaim the world well lost. It is hard to imagine that either possibility ever crossed Emily Brontë's mind, for either would destroy the pattern of her book, but her rejection of them is a measure of her moral and artistic power. For instead of its conventional potentialities the scene acquires an astonishing moral power. Heathcliff confronted with the dying Catherine, is ruthless, morally ruthless: instead of easy comfort he offers her a brutal analysis of what she has done.

> "You teach me now how cruel you've been—cruel and false. *Why* did you despise me? *Why* did you betray your own heart Cathy? I have not one word of comfort. You deserve this. You have killed yourself. Yes, you may kiss me, and cry: and wring out my kisses and tears: they'll blight you—they'll damn you. You loved me—then what *right* had you to leave me? What right—answer me —for the poor fancy you felt for Linton? Because misery and degradation, and death, and nothing that God or Satan could inflict would have parted us, *you,* of your own will, did it. I have not broken your heart—*you* have broken it; and in breaking it you have broken mine. So much the worse that I am strong. Do I want to live? What kind of living will it be when you—oh, God! would *you* like to live with your soul in the grave?" [11]

It is one of the harshest passages in all literature, but it is also one of the most moving. For the brutality is not neurotic, nor sadistic, nor romantic. The Catherine-Heathcliff relationship, standing as it does for a humanity finer and more morally profound than the standards of the Lintons and Earnshaws has to undergo

[11] *Ibid.,* Chap. XV.

the kind of examination Heathcliff here brings to it. Anything less, anything which smudged or sweetened the issues involved, would be inadequate, unworthy. Heathcliff knows that nothing can save Catherine from death but that one thing alone can give her peace, a full and utterly honest understanding and acceptance of their relationship and what it implies. There is no hope in comfort or compromise. Any such weakness would debase them both and make a futile waste of their lives and death. For Heathcliff and Catherine, who reject the Lintons' chapel roof and the consolations of Christianity, know, too, that their relationship is more important than death.

In the section of the book that follows Catherine's death Heathcliff continues the revenge he has begun with his marriage to Isabella. It is the most peculiar section of the novel and the most difficult because the quality of Heathcliff's feeling is of a kind most of us find hard to comprehend. All normal and healthy human feeling is rejected. He cries:

> "I have no pity! I have no pity! The more the worms writhe, the more I yearn to crush out their entrails! It is a moral teething; and I grind with greater energy, in proportion to the increase of pain." [12]

"It is a moral teething"—the phrase is both odd and significant, giving as it does the answer to our temptation to treat this whole section as a delineation of pathological neurosis. Heathcliff becomes a monster: what he does to Isabella, to Hareton, to Cathy, to his son, even to the wretched Hindley, is cruel and inhuman beyond normal thought. He seems concerned to achieve new refinements of horror, new depths of degradation. And we tend to feel, perhaps, unless we read with full care and responsiveness, that Emily Brontë has gone too far, that the revenge (especially the marriage of Cathy and Linton Heathcliff) has o'erflown the measure.

And yet it is only one side of our minds, the conscious, limited side that refers what we are reading to our everyday measures of experience that makes this objection. Another side, which is more completely responding to Emily Brontë's art, is carried on. And the astonishing achievement of this part of the book is that, despite our protests about probability (protests which, incidentally, a good deal of twentieth-century history makes a little complacent), despite everything he does and is, we continue to sympathize with Heathcliff —not, obviously, to admire him or defend him, but to give him

---

[12] *Ibid.*, Chap. XIV.

our inmost sympathy, to continue in an obscure way to identify ourselves with him *against* the other characters.

The secret of this achievement lies in such a phrase as "it is a moral teething" and in the gradually clarifying pattern of the book. Heathcliff's revenge may involve a pathological condition of hatred, but it is not at bottom merely neurotic. It has a moral force. For what Heathcliff does is to use against his enemies with complete ruthlessness their own weapons, to turn on them (stripped of their romantic veils) their own standards, to beat them at their own game. The weapons he uses against the Earnshaws and Lintons are their own weapons of money and arranged marriages. He gets power over them by the classic methods of the ruling class, expropriation and property deals. He buys out Hindley and reduces him to drunken impotency, he marries Isabella and then organizes the marriage of his son to Catherine Linton, so that the entire property of the two families shall be controlled by himself. He systematically degrades Hareton Earnshaw to servility and illiteracy. "I want the triumph of seeing *my* descendant fairly lord of *their* estates! My child hiring their children to till their father's lands for wages." [13] (This is a novel which, some critics will tell you, has nothing to do with anything as humdrum as society or life as it is actually lived.) And what particularly tickles Heathcliff's fancy is his achievement of the supreme ruling-class triumph of making Hareton, the boy he degrades, feel a deep and even passionate attachment towards himself.

Heathcliff retains our sympathy throughout this dreadful section of the book because instinctively we recognize a rough moral justice in what he has done to his oppressors and because, though he is inhuman, we understand *why* he is inhuman. Obviously we do not approve of what he does, but we understand it; the deep and complex issues behind his actions are revealed to us. We recognize that the very forces which drove him to rebellion for a higher freedom have themselves entrapped him in their own values and determined the nature of his revenge.

If *Wuthering Heights* were to stop at this point it would still be a great book, but a wholly sombre and depressing one. Man would be revealed as inevitably caught up in the meshes of his own creating; and against the tragic horror of Heathcliff's appalling rebellion the limited but complacent world of Thrushcross Grange would seem a tempting haven and the novel would resolve itself

[13] *Ibid.*, Chap. XX.

into the false antithesis of Thrushcross Grange/Wuthering Heights, just as in *Oliver Twist* the real antithesis becomes sidetracked into the false one of Brownlow/Fagin. But *Wuthering Heights,* a work of supreme and astonishing genius, does not stop here. We have not done with Heathcliff yet.

For at the moment of his horrible triumph a change begins to come over Heathcliff.

> "It is a poor conclusion, is it not?" he observed, having brooded a while on the scene he had just witnessed: "an absurd termination to my violent exertions? I get levers and mattocks to demolish the two houses, and train myself to be capable of working like Hercules, and when everything is ready and in my power, I find the will to lift a slate off either roof has vanished! My old enemies have not beaten me; now would be the precise time to revenge myself on their representatives: I could do it, and none could hinder me. But where is the use? I don't care for striking; I can't take the trouble to raise my hand! That sounds as if I had been labouring the whole time only to exhibit a fine trait of magnanimity. It is far from being the case: I have lost the faculty of enjoying their destruction, and I am too idle to destroy for nothing.
>
> "Nelly, there is a strange change approaching: I'm in its shadow at present." [14]

And he goes on to speak of Cathy and Hareton, who "seemed a personification of my youth, not a human being." "Hareton's aspect was the ghost of my immortal love; of my wild endeavour to hold my right; my degradation, my pride, my happiness and my anguish." When Nelly asks "But what do you mean by a *change,* Mr. Heathcliff?" he can only answer "I shall not know that till it comes . . . I'm only half conscious of it now." Once more the stage is set for a familiar scene, the conversion of the wicked who will in the final chapter turn from his wickedness. And once more the conventional must look again.

The change that comes over Heathcliff and the novel and leads us on to the wonderful, quiet, gentle, tentative evocation of nature in the final sentence, is a very subtle one. It has something of the quality of the last two acts of *The Winter's Tale* but is much less complete, less confident. Mr. Klingopulos in his interesting essay on *Wuthering Heights*[15] has commented on the ambiguous nature of this final tranquillity. I do not agree with his analysis but he has

[14] *Ibid.,* Chap. XXXIII.
[15] *Scrutiny,* Vol. XIV, No. 4.

caught the tone most convincingly. Heathcliff, watching the love of
Cathy and Hareton grow, comes to understand something of the
failure of his own revenge. As Cathy teaches Hareton to write and
stops laughing at his ignorance we too are taken back to the first
Catherine.

Cathy and Hareton are not in the novel an easy re-creation of
Catherine and Heathcliff; they are, as Mr. Klingopulos remarks,
different people, even lesser people, certainly people conceived on
a less intense and passionate scale than the older lovers. But they
do symbolize the continuity of life and human aspirations, and it
is through them that Heathcliff comes to understand the hollow-
ness of his triumph. It is when Hareton, who loves him, comes to
Cathy's aid when he strikes her that the full meaning of his own
relationship with Catherine comes back to him and he becomes
aware that in the feeling between Cathy and Hareton there is
something of the same quality. From the moment that Cathy and
Hareton are drawn together as rebels the change begins. For now
for the first time Heathcliff is confronted not with those who
accept the values of Wuthering Heights and Thrushcross Grange
but with those who share, however remotely, his own wild en-
deavours to hold his right.

Heathcliff does not repent. Nelly tries to make him turn to the
consolations of religion.

> "You are aware, Mr. Heathcliff," I said, "that from the time
> you were thirteen years old, you have lived a selfish, unchristian
> life; and probably hardly had a Bible in your hands during all that
> period. You must have forgotten the contents of the Book, and you
> may not have space to search it now. Could it be hurtful to send for
> some one—some minister of any denomination, it does not matter
> which—to explain it, and show you how very far you have erred
> from its precepts; and how unfit you will be for its heaven, unless a
> change takes place before you die?"
> "I'm rather obliged than angry, Nelly," he said, "for you remind
> me of the manner in which I desire to be buried. It is to be carried
> to the churchyard in the evening. You and Hareton may, if you
> please, accompany me: and mind, particularly, to notice that the
> sexton obeys my directions concerning the two coffins! No minister
> need come; nor need anything be said over me.—I tell you I have
> nearly attained my heaven, and that of others is altogether unvalued
> and uncoveted by me." [16]

[16] *Wuthering Heights,* Chap. XXXIV.

One sentence here, in its limpid simplicity, especially evokes the state of mind Heathcliff has come to. He speaks of the manner in which he wishes to be buried. "It is to be carried to the church-yard in the evening." The great rage has died in him. He has come to see the pointlessness of his fight to revenge himself on the world of power and property through its own values. Just as Catherine had to face the full moral horror of her betrayal of their love, he must face the full horror of his betrayal too. And once he has faced it he can die, not nobly or triumphantly, but at least as a man, leaving with Cathy and Hareton the possibility of carrying on the struggle he has begun, and in his death he will achieve again human dignity, "to be carried to the churchyard in the evening."

It is this re-achievement of manhood by Heathcliff, an under-standing reached with no help from the world he despises, which, together with the developing relationship of Cathy and Hareton and the sense of the continuity of life in nature, gives to the last pages of *Wuthering Heights* a sense of positive and unsentimental hope. The Catherine-Heathcliff relationship has been vindicated. Life will go on and others will rebel against the oppressors. Nothing has been solved but much has been experienced. Lies, complacencies and errors, appalling errors, have been revealed. A veil has been drawn from the conventional face of bourgeois man; he has been revealed, through Heathcliff, without his mask.

Above all, the quality of the feeling that binds Catherine and Heathcliff has been conveyed to us. Their love, which Heathcliff can without idealism call immortal, is something beyond the in-dividualist dream of two soul-mates finding full realization in one another; it is an expression of the necessity of man, if he is to choose life rather than death, to revolt against all that would destroy his inmost needs and aspirations, of the necessity of all human beings to become, through acting together, more fully human. Catherine, responding to this deep human necessity, rebels with Heathcliff but in marrying Edgar (a 'good' marriage if ever there was one) betrays her own humanity; Heathcliff, by revenging himself on the tyrants through the adoption of their own standards makes more clear those standards but betrays too his humanity and destroys his relationship with the dead Catherine whose spirit must haunt the moors in terror and dismay.

Only when the new change has come over Heathcliff and he again recognizes through Hareton (and remotely, therefore, through Cathe-rine herself) the full claims of humanity can Catherine be released from torment and their relationship re-established. Death is a matter of little importance in *Wuthering Heights* because the issues the novel is concerned with are greater than the individual life and death. The deaths of Catherine and Heathcliff are indeed a kind of triumph because ultimately each faces death honestly, keeping faith. But there is no suggestion that death itself is a triumph: on the contrary it is life that asserts itself, continues, blossoms again.

Mr. David Wilson in his excellent essay on Emily Brontë [17] to which I am deeply indebted (though I do not agree with all of his interpretation) suggests an identification, not necessarily conscious in Emily Brontë's mind, of Heathcliff with the rebellious working men of the hungry 'forties' and of Catherine with that part of the educated class which felt compelled to identify itself with their cause. Such a formulation, suggestive as it is, seems to me to be too far removed from the actual impact of *Wuthering Heights* as a novel, to be satisfactory. But Mr. Wilson has done a valuable service in rescuing *Wuthering Heights* from the transcendentalists and in insisting on the place of Haworth (generally assumed to be a remote country village) in the industrial revolution and its attendant social unrest.[18] The value of his suggestion with regard to Heathcliff and Catherine seems to me in the emphasis it gives to the concrete, local particularity of the book.

It is very necessary to be reminded that just as the values of Wuthering Heights and Thrushcross Grange are not simply the values of *any* tyranny but specifically those of Victorian society, so is the rebellion of Heathcliff a particular rebellion, that of the worker physically and spiritually degraded by the conditions and relationships of this same society. That Heathcliff ceases to be one of the exploited is true, but it is also true that just in so far as he adopts (with a ruthlessness that frightens even the ruling class itself) the standards of the ruling class, so do the human values implicit in his early rebellion and in his love for Catherine vanish. All that is involved in the Catherine–Heathcliff relationship, all that it stands for in human needs and hopes, can be realized only through the active rebellion of the oppressed.

Wuthering Heights then is an expression in the imaginative terms of art of the stresses and tensions and conflicts, personal and spiritual, of nineteenth-century capitalist society. It is a novel with-

[17] *Modern Quarterly*, Miscellany No. 1 (1947).
[18] One of the most interesting exhibits in the Haworth museum today is a proclamation of the Queen ordering the reading of the Riot Act against the rebellious workers of the West Riding.

out idealism, without false comforts, without any implication that power over their destinies rests outside the struggles and actions of human beings themselves. Its powerful evocation of nature, of moorland and storm, of the stars and seasons is an essential part of its revelation of the very movement of life itself. The men and women of *Wuthering Heights* are not the prisoners of nature; they live in the world and strive to change it, sometimes successfully, always painfully, with almost infinite difficulty and error.

This unending struggle, of which the struggle to advance from class society to the higher humanity of a classless world is but an episode, is conveyed to us in *Wuthering Heights* precisely because the novel is conceived in actual, concrete, particular terms, because the quality of oppression revealed in the novel is not abstract but concrete, not vague but particular. And that is why Emily Brontë's novel is at the same time a statement about the life she knew, the life of Victorian England, and a statement about life as such. Virginia Woolf, writing about it, said:

> That gigantic ambition is to be felt throughout the novel, a struggle half thwarted but of superb conviction, to say something through the mouths of characters which is not merely "I love" or "I hate" but "we, the whole human race" and "You; the eternal powers . . ." the sentence remains unfinished." [19]

I do not think it remains unfinished.

[19] *The Common Reader* (Pelican ed.), p. 158.

Fiction and the Matrix of Analogy

by Mark Schorer

Wuthering Heights, as I understand it, means to be a work of edification: Emily Brontë begins by wishing to instruct her narrator, the dandy, Lockwood, in the nature of a grand passion; she ends by instructing herself in the vanity of human wishes. She means to dramatize with something like approval—the phrase that follows is from *Middlemarch*—"the sense of a stupendous self and an insignificant world." What her metaphors signify is the impermanence of self and the permanence of something larger.

To exalt the power of human feeling, Emily Brontë roots her analogies in the fierce life of animals and in the relentless life of the elements—fire, wind, water. "Wuthering," we are told, is "a significant provincial adjective, descriptive of the atmospheric tumult to which its station is exposed in stormy weather," and, immediately after, that "one may guess the power of the north wind blowing over the edge, by the excessive slant of a few stunted firs at the end of the house; and by a range of gaunt thorns all stretching their limbs one way, as if craving alms of the sun." The application of this landscape to the characters is made explicit in the second half of the novel, when Heathcliff says, "Now, my bonny lad, you are *mine!* And we'll see if one tree won't grow as crooked as another, with the same wind to twist it!" This analogy provides at least half of the metaphorical base of the novel.

Human conditions are like the activities of the landscape, where rains *flood,* blasts *wail,* and the snow and wind *whirl wildly* and *blow* out lights. A serving woman *heaves* "like a sea after a high wind"; a preacher "*poured* forth his zeal in a *shower*"; Mrs. Dean *rushes* to welcome Lockwood, "exclaiming *tumultuously*"; spirits are "at high-water mark"; Linton's soul is as different from Heath-

---

"Fiction and the Matrix of Analogy," from Kenyon Review, XI, *4 (September, 1949). Copyright 1949 by* Kenyon Review. *Reprinted by permission of* Kenyon Review *and Mark Schorer.*

cliff's "as a moonbeam from lightning, or frost from fire"; abuse is *lavished* in a *torrent,* or *pours forth* in a *deluge;* illnesses are *"weathered* . . . through"; "sensations" are felt in a *gush;* "your veins are *full* of *ice water;* but mine are *boiling";* hair *flies,* bodies *toss* or *tremble* like reeds, tears *stream* or *rain down* among the ashes; discord and distress arise in a *tumult;* Catherine Linton "was *struck* during a *tempest* of passion with a kind of fit" and *"flew off* in the *height* of it."

Faces, too, are like landscapes: "a *cloud* of meditation" hangs over Nelly Dean's *"ruddy* countenance"; Catherine had "a suddenly *clouded* brow; her humor was a mere *vane* for constantly varying caprices"; "the surface of" the boy Heathcliff's "face and hands was dismally *beclouded"* with dirt; later, his face *"brightened* for a moment; then it was *overcast* afresh." "His forehead . . . *shaded* over with a heavy *cloud";* and "the *clouded* windows of hell," his eyes, *"flashed."* Hareton, likewise, grows "black as a *thundercloud";* or *darkens* with a frown. The older Catherine experienced whole *"seasons* of gloom," and the younger Catherine's "heart was *clouded* . . . in double *darkness."* Her "face was just like the *landscape— shadows* and *sunshine* flitting over it in rapid succession; but the *shadows* rested longer, and the *sunshine* was more transient." Sometimes "her eyes are *radiant* with *cloudless* pleasure," and at the end, Hareton shakes off "the *clouds* of ignorance and degradation," and his *"brightening* mind *brightened* his features."

Quite as important as the imagery of wind and cloud and water is the imagery of fire. In every interior, the fire on the hearth is the center of pictorial interest, and the characters sit *"burning* their eyes out before the fire." Eyes *burn* with anguish but do not *melt;* they always *flash* and *sparkle.* Fury *kindles,* temper *kindles,* a *"spark* of spirit" *kindles.* Catherine has a *fiery* disposition, but so do objects and states: words *brand,* shame is *burning,* merriment *expires* quickly, fevers *consume* life; hot coffee and basins *smoke,* they do not steam; and Isabella shrieks "as if witches were running *red-hot* needles into her." Sometimes fire is identified with other elements, as when a servant urges *"flakes* of *flame* up the chimney," or when Isabella complains that the fire causes the wound on her neck, first stopped by the icy cold, to stream and smart.

Metaphors of earth—earth takes more solid and durable forms than the other elements—are interestingly few. Twice Heathcliff is likened to "an arid wilderness of *furze* and *whinstone";* there is a reference to his *"flinty* gratification"; and once he speaks scornfully of "the *soil* of" Linton's "shallow cares." Earth and vegetation

sometimes result in a happy juxtaposition of the vast or the violent
and the little or the homely, as when Heathcliff says of Linton that
"He might as well plant *an oak in a flowerpot*," or when he threatens
to "crush his ribs in like *a rotten hazelnut*," which is like his saying
that Catherine's passion could be as readily encompassed by Linton
as "*the sea* could be . . . contained in that *horse-trough*."

Most of the animals are wild. Hareton's "whiskers encroached
bearishly over his cheeks," and Heathcliff denies the paternity of
"that bear." Hareton had been "cast out like an unfledged *dun-
nock*," and Heathcliff is a "fierce, pitiless, *wolfish* man." He is
also "a *bird* of bad omen" and "an evil *beast*" prowling between
a "stray *sheep*" "and the fold, waiting his time to spring and destroy." He has a "*ferocious* gaze" and a *savage* utterance; he *growls*
and *howls* "like a beast," and is many times named "a brute," "a
beast," "a brute beast." He struggles like a *bear,* he has *sharp
cannibal teeth* which *gleam* "through the dark," and "*basilisk* eyes
. . . *quenched* by sleeplessness." He *gnashes* his teeth and *foams*
like a *mad dog*. He is "like a *bull*" to Linton's "*lamb*," and only
at the very end, the exhausted end, "he breathed as fast as a *cat*."

For the domestic and the gentler animals are generally used for
purposes of harsh satire or vilification. Edgar, "the soft thing,"
"possessed the power to depart, as much as a *cat* possesses the power
to leave a *mouse* half killed, or a *bird* half eaten." He is "not a
lamb" but "a sucking *leveret*," and his sister is a "pitiful, slavish,
mean-minded *brach*," she is among those *worms,* who, "the more
they writhe, the more" Heathcliff yearns "to crush out their en-
trails." Hindley dies in a stupor, "snorting like a *horse*"; flaying
and scalping" would not have roused him, and when the doctor
arrives, "the *beast* has changed to *carrion*." Hareton is "an infernal
calf," and young Linton is a "*puling chicken*" and a "*whelp*." Like
a dying dog, he "slowly *trailed* himself off, and lay down," or, like
a cold one, he "*shrank* closer to the fire." He "had *shrunk* into a
corner of the settle, as quiet as a *mouse*"; he is called "a little per-
ishing *monkey*"; and he "achieved his exit exactly as a *spaniel*
might." He is also "an abject *reptile*" and "a *cockatrice*." Hareton,
who is capable on occasion of gathering "*venom* with reflection,"
is once called a "*magpie*," and once said to be "obstinate as a
mule"—one of the few kindly animal references in the novel.
To be sure, Isabella describes herself as though she were a deer:
"I *bounded, leaped* and *flew* down the steep road; then . . . *shot*
direct across the moor, *rolling* over banks, and *wading* through
marshes." And Catherine, on the whole, is not abused. She is a

"cunning little *fox*" and she runs "like a *mouse*," but chiefly she is "soft and mild as a *dove*."

Emily Brontë's metaphors color all her diction. As her epithets are charged with passion—"jealous guardianship," "vexatious phlegm," "importunate branch"—so her verbs are verbs of violent movement and conflict, both contributing to a rhetorical texture where everything is at a pitch from which it can only subside. The verbs *demand* exhaustion, just as the metaphors *demand* rest. And there is an antithetical chorus in this rhetoric, a contrapuntal warning, which, usually but not only in the voice of Nelly Dean, says, "Hush! Hush!" all through the novel, at the beginning of paragraph after paragraph. At the end, everything *is* hushed. And the moths *fluttering* over Heathcliff's grave and "the soft wind *breathing* through the grass" that grows on it have at last more power than he, for all his passion. These soft and fragile things paradoxically endure.

The passions of animals, if we may speak of them as passions, have meaning in that they are presumably necessary to survival; Heathcliff's passion destroys others, himself, and at last, itself. The tumult of the elements alternates with periods of peace, and the seasons are not only autumn and winter. The *fact* of alternation enables nature to endure. The singleness of Heathcliff's tempestuous and wintery emotional life dooms it. Thus there is a curious and ironic contrast between the condition and the destiny of Heathcliff, and the full facts of those areas of metaphor. When, at the end of the novel, Nelly remarks that "the same moon shone through the window; and the same autumn landscape lay outside" as eighteen years before, she is speaking with metaphorical accuracy; but Heathcliff is *not* the same. He has not indeed come into a "sober, disenchanted maturity"—that will be the privilege of Hareton and the second Cathy; but he has completely changed in the fashion that Joseph described much earlier—"so as by fire." ". . . there is a strange change approaching: I'm in its shadow at present," he declares when he has found that nothing is worth the feeling of it. At last, after all the windy tumult and the tempests, he says, "I have to remind myself to *breathe*. . . ."

If his life, exhausted at the end, has not been, as he once said of it, "a moral teething," and the novel, therefore, no tragedy, the story of his life has been a moral teething for the author. Lockwood is instructed in the nature of a grand passion, but he and Emily Brontë together are instructed in its final fruits: even roaring fires end in a bed of ashes. Her metaphors instruct her, and her verbs. That besides these rhetorical means (which in their functioning make tolerable the almost impossibly inflated style), she should have found structural means as well which give her whole narrative the remote quality of a twice-told tale, the property of an old wife (and so make its melodrama endurable), should reinforce the point. At the end, the voice that drones on is the perdurable voice of the country, Nelly Dean's. No more than Heathcliff did Emily Brontë quite intend that homespun finality. Like the older Catherine, Emily Brontë could have said of her book, "I've dreamed in my life dreams that have stayed with me ever after, and changed my ideas: they've gone through and through me, like wine through water, and altered the color of my mind." Her rhetoric altered the form of her intention. It is her education; it shapes her insight.

The Brontë Sisters and *Wuthering Heights*

by Derek Traversi

A notable difference in imaginative quality separates the novels of Charlotte and Emily Brontë from those of the other great English novelists of the last century. The difference appears to be one of emotional intensity, the product of a unique concentration upon fundamental human passions in a state approaching essential purity. Whether this concentration is compatible with the nature of the novel—and there has been a tendency to regard the work of the Brontës as something of a "sport", [1] a remarkable oddity in literary history—is no doubt open to discussion. Many of the great novelists of the period—Dickens, Thackeray, George Eliot—showed moral preoccupations and social interests more explicit than those revealed in *Wuthering Heights*. We may readily agree that the range of these writers is wider, their points of contact with the human scene more intensively portrayed; but when this has been allowed, there remains to be taken into account an astonishing mixture of romantic commonplace and personal inspiration, primitive feeling and spiritual exaltation, which corresponds to potentialities of human nature otherwise unduly concealed during this period.

It is easy to feel at times, in reading Charlotte Brontë, that contact with the outside world served only to disperse a gift, the true strength of which lay rather in concentrated vision. In Emily (1818–48), whose excursions into that world were brief and followed invariably by a return to the true sources of her inspiration, that vision was preserved in essential purity. The poems she wrote afford a glimpse into the fiercely maintained integrity of her emotions. This is not to say that they are lacking in conventional romantic

---

[1] F. R. Leavis uses the word in *The Great Tradition* (London, 1948).

attributes. By-products in great part of the dream world in which
the sisters lived, creating in close collaboration the interminable
Gondal romances of their unusually protracted adolescence, they
came to life whenever Emily's own peculiarly spiritual passion il-
luminates what would otherwise be commonplace:

> Cheerful is the hearth, soft the matted floor;
> Not one shivering gust creeps through pane or door;
> The little lamp burns straight, its rays shoot strong and far:
> I trim it well, to be the wanderer's guiding-star.

The cheerful comforts of the home, associated no doubt with the
long winter months at Haworth, are seen here as the background for
an expression of strength, of confident adherence to what are felt
already to be sources of intimate fortitude. The lamp, "little" though
it is, "burns straight," its rays are "strong and clear"; and this being
so, in the last stages of the poem concentration is rewarded by true
spiritual vision:

> What I love shall come like visitant of air,
> Safe in secret power from lurking human snare,
> What loves me, no word of mine shall e'er betray,
> Though for faith unstained my life must forfeit pay.

> Burn, then little lamp; glimmer straight and clear—
> Hush! a rustling wing stirs, methinks, the air;
> He for whom I wait, thus ever comes to me;
> Strange Power! I trust thy might; trust thou my constancy.
>
> *(The Visionary)*

In verses such as these, inner seclusion of spirit, not dissipated by
contact with the outer world, becomes a true source of strength.
Traces of an inferior rhetoric survive, no doubt, in "lurking human
snare" and even in the "faith unstained" opposed to it;[2] but the
assertion of that faith has a personal force which transcends its
literary origin. The visitant from the world of spirit manifests
itself intimately in "secret power," and rouses a response in equally
intimate dedication. That dedication, like the lamp on the hearth
which serves as a focal point for affection and fellowship, burns
"straight and clear," and its felt power, or "might," evokes in
answer a trustful "constancy." Here, beneath the superficial at-

---

[2] Rhetorical, too, in its effect, though clearly the work of no ordinary personality, is the greater part of the famous *No coward soul is mine*, described
by Charlotte as "the last lines my sister Emily ever wrote."

tributes of romantic sentiment, we are in touch with the true
sources of strength that determine the Brontë vision.

Only in *Wuthering Heights* (1847) does this strength find complete and consistent expression. To say this is not to deny that
there are paragraphs in which the presence of incidental faults makes
itself felt in the narration, moments in which the creative impulse,
instead of burning clearly, seems to smoulder or die down. A simple
account of the story of the orphan Heathcliff, his love for Catherine
Earnshaw, and the revenge which he obtains through his marriage
with Isabella Linton upon those who have deprived him of his
proper satisfactions in life, would go far to justify a reading of the
novel as simply one more example of a familiar romantic type;
an example perhaps more coherent in design and execution than
most of its kind, but still a mixture of brutal melodrama and
exaggerated sentiment. To trace a literary creation to its formal
origins, however, is not necessarily to define its true character. Given
the circumstances of Emily Brontë's life, it was natural that the
commonplaces of romantic inspiration should play a great part in
her novel; but a clear examination of the writing, the treatment of
the subjects, proves conclusively that its true significance lies in
the transformation of this romanticism through the operation of
an intensely personal imaginative power.

No nineteenth-century novel, indeed, is less derivative in its essential content, or answers more fully to an intimate vision. In its
fundamental as distinct from its accidental qualities, *Wuthering
Heights* is an exploration of human passion at different levels and
of the effect exercised by the interplay of these levels upon human
life in its individual and social aspects alike. Creative or destructive
in their consequences, making for life or death, basic human emotions are presented in a state of purity and concentration; no other
novel of the Victorian period has penetrated so far into the depths of
passion, or followed with such unrelenting logic to their ultimate
consequences the intensity of its operations. The very novelty of the
enterprise accounts for the remoteness of the book, at its most success-
ful moments, from the greater part of the normal devices of the
novelist. The novel, as Emily Brontë's great contemporaries conceived it, dealt primarily with the analysis of characters in their
mutual relationships and in their attitude to external events; but
the beings who dominate *Wuthering Heights* draw their life from
sources at once simpler and deeper, more obscure and less differentiated, than those with which the novel is traditionally concerned.
Purged of all accidental qualities, indivisible in essence and too

self-consistent to undergo change, their function is that of elements
which can only, in their relations with the similar entities around
them, destroy or suffer destruction. The result is a unique imaginative creation which, largely ignoring the moral and social assumptions of the contemporary novel, aspires rather to the severe
simplicity of ancient tragedy.

The presence of the distinctive power which animates *Wuthering
Heights* is felt whenever the emotions of the chief characters are
deeply involved. No doubt there are moments—as when Catherine
is described "dashing her head against the arm of the sofa, and
grinding her teeth so that you might fancy she would crash them
to splinters"—when passion fails to make its presence felt through
the crudity of its expression; but they are not, taken by and large,
characteristic. The romantic melodramas with which Emily Brontë
was certainly familiar owed their success almost invariably to effects
created by ambiguity and mistiness, to lack of precision and vague
suggestiveness. Romantic emotion of this type is felt rather than
seen, is always rather a possibility than a tangible reality. In
Wuthering Heights, the exact opposite normally occurs. Although
the events described may frequently strike us as incredible, they
are related in the great majority of cases with vivid clarity and precision. The qualities by which the writing is differentiated from
the commonplaces of romantic sensibility are nowhere more apparent than in the opening description of Heathcliff's house and its
surroundings. Wuthering Heights is described, as the narrator Mr.
Lockwood sees it, through a series of exact, vivid touches. The
exposition, careful, orderly, and even slightly pedantic, as befits
the speaker, rises almost imperceptibly to the deeply poetic reference
to "the range of gaunt thorns all stretching their limbs one way, as if
craving alms of the sun," so that this evocation of the spirit of
place does not strike the reader in any way as an intrusion. Above
all, the temptation to exploit the poetic note is firmly resisted and
the description of the interior which follows, where firmness in
the grasp of detail and the stress laid on the normality of the
setting ("The apartment and furniture would have been nothing
extraordinary as belonging to a homely northern farmer") belongs
to a type of writing diametrically opposed to romantic sensationalism. The same concrete imagination makes itself felt even in
Lockwood's account of his highly theatrical dream, where if anywhere we might have expected the strained romantic note to impose
a lack of precision, but where, in fact, the illusion of reality is maintained through a sense of physical pain that borders on the in-

From a profound sense of the finite and dependent nature of man ("surely you and everybody have a notion that there is or should be an existence of yours beyond you"), there arises the desire to make contact with a reality by which the self may be completed. In the light of this desire the world of mere external presentation—in so far as it remains merely external, unrelated to the spiritual intuition born of this consuming metaphysical passion--appears empty, and the very sense of this emptiness can properly be related to an experience of religious desolation: "If all else perished, and *he* remained, I should still continue to be; and if all else remained, and he were annihilated, the universe would turn to a mighty stranger: I should not seem a part of it."

The consequences of the emotion so expressed extend, in the contrast which the novel so consistently stresses between Heathcliff and Linton, and between Catherine's feelings for them both, to the moral order. Linton may be held, in a certain sense, to symbolize the superficial graces of civilized life, in which Heathcliff is totally lacking. It is perfectly natural that Catherine should be attracted to Linton. Courtesy, charm, and urbanity are all qualities worthy to be admired, and it is on their account that she is, at a certain level of her nature, impelled to respond to Linton's affection; but, as she herself recognizes, it is not the deepest part of her nature which is thus involved: "My love for Linton is like the foliage in the woods: time will change it, I'm well aware, as winter changes the trees. My love for Heathcliff resembles the eternal rocks beneath: a source of little visible delight, but *necessary*." Once more the conflict between two types of feeling is stated with a simplicity fundamentally intellectual in its sense of definition, which emphasizes the absence of all purely transitory or sentimental considerations. In the contrast between the *agreeable* and the *necessary*, between emotions which serve at best to adorn life and others whose absence is felt to be equivalent to spiritual death, we can observe once more the peculiar inspiration of the book, and our judgment of it as a whole is likely to depend upon our reaction to these words.

It is not surprising that this reaction has differed notably from reader to reader. Behind such passionate utterances as this of Catherine there lies a moral problem of the utmost seriousness. This problem follows from the presence in *Wuthering Heights* of the spiritual content whose nature we have just indicated, and Emily Brontë was perfectly conscious that it existed. We feel its presence clearly when we follow, through the eyes of Nelly Dean, whose common sense offers throughout a necessary counterweight, a rele-

vant though not a final comment,[3] the process of reasoning by which
Catherine is urged to abandon Heathcliff. Reflection, aided by
Nelly, presents Heathcliff as what he undeniably is: a brutal creature
whom she could certainly abandon with social advantage to marry
the young, rich, and attractive Edgar Linton. Nelly, guided by her
inherent good nature and by her long if not particularly imaginative experience of life, maintains that Edgar is a good match, that he
is, socially speaking, acceptable and likely to bring her to normal
domestic happiness, whereas her devotion to Heathcliff can only end
in disaster and degradation. All this is undoubtedly true, relevant to
the complete understanding of a novel which presents the destructive
consequences, as well as the transforming ecstacies, of passion; but
the impressive simplicity of Catherine's reply is sufficient evidence
that it is not all the truth. "He" [Heathcliff] "is more myself than I
am. Whatever our souls are made of, his and mine are the same; and
Linton's is as different as a moonbeam from lightning, or frost from
fire." Once more, we are conscious of being raised from normal social
considerations to the world of essential passions with which, in their
transforming and destructive operation, Emily Brontë is finally
concerned.

Considered in the light of the central passion which thus animates
the novel, it becomes easier to respond to its second main theme:
that conveyed in the contrast between the two houses which between
them divide the action, Wuthering Heights and Thrushcross Grange.
Wuthering Heights clearly reflects the character of Heathcliff, who
owns it; we might, indeed, call Heathcliff its human incarnation.
Severe, gloomy, and brutal in aspect and atmosphere, firmly rooted
in local tradition and custom, it is an appropriate background for the
life of bare and primitive passion to which its owner is dedicated.
Thrushcross Grange, the home of the Lintons, is in every respect
different. It reflects a conception of life at first sight altogether more
agreeable, more human than that set against it; a conception, indeed,
which can attract the approval of Nelly Dean's common sense and so
is not to be despised, but which, when closely observed, shows signs
of decadence. Like Wuthering Heights, though with very different
results, Thrushcross Grange answers to the character of its owners.
Judged from a superficial standpoint, the Lintons seem to possess

[3] Her reaction to the expression, just quoted, of Catherine's need for Heathcliff is typical, and, so far as it goes, relevant: "If I can make any sense of your
nonsense, Miss," I said, "it only goes to convince me that you are ignorant of
the duties you undertake in marrying; or else that you are a wicked, un-
principled girl."

refinement, kindness, an amiability which makes life tolerable; but a closer inspection shows that the exclusion of Heathcliff's intense if self-concerning passion is not altogether a proof of moral strength. Beneath the surface of refinement exhibited by the Lintons in their ancestral surroundings exist moral flaws which play a part of the utmost importance in the development of the tragedy.

There is in the early pages of the novel a most significant moment in which Thrushcross Grange and those who dwell in it are seen from the outside, from the standpoint of external and critical observers. At this moment Heathcliff and Catherine, still young children, climb up—acutely aware of themselves as intruders—to look into the illuminated windows of the Linton mansion. Their first glimpse of this strange new world produces an impression of contemptuous hostility which will always remain with them. They observe that the Linton children, far from feeling happy in their luxurious home, are in fact quarrelling bitterly over a lap-dog, itself a symbol of pampered indulgence, which each desires to handle and pet:

> "And now, guess what your good children were doing? Isabella—
> I believe she is eleven, a year younger than Cathy—lay screaming at
> the farther end of the room, shrieking as if witches were running
> red-hot needles into her. Edgar stood on the hearth weeping silently,
> and in the middle of the table sat a little dog, shaking its paw and
> yelping; which, from their mutual accusations, we understood they
> had nearly pulled in two between them. The idiots! That was their
> pleasure! to quarrel who should hold a heap of warm hair, and
> each begin to cry because both, after struggling to get it, refused to
> take it. We laughed outright at the petted things; we did despise
> them!"

The contempt apparent in Heathcliff's words represents the attitude of a soul in which the fundamental passions are still intensely alive for a world which claims to be superior but is in reality trivial, selfish, and empty. The emphasis laid upon the soft and clinging luxury in which the Lintons live, protected by bull-dogs and obsequious servants from the intrusion of the inferior world outside, is calculated to produce an impression of excessive sweetness and decay: "We saw—ah! it was beautiful—a splendid place carpeted with crimson, and crimson-covered chairs and tables, and a pure white ceiling bordered by gold, a shower of glass-drops hanging in silver chains from the centre, and shimmering with little soft tapers." The sight of so much luxury undoubtedly makes a certain appeal to the children, strikes them from outside as "beautiful." It corresponds, indeed, to a sense of social graciousness which the Heathcliff world is the poorer for lacking; but it also rouses in the youthful intruders from this other world a feeling of repudiation which the behavior of the dwellers in this "paradise" can only intensify. The "gold," the crimson carpets and chair-coverings which serve to deaden, to mollify the impact of life, the slightly unreal prettiness of the "shower of glass-drops hanging in silver chains," and the barely defined sense of exquisite decadence in the reference to the "little soft tapers" burning in the room: all these, seen through eyes already dedicated to passionate sincerity, point to a contrast which lies at the very heart of the novel.

The contrast, indeed, is carried in similar terms into the main body of the story. When Catherine, as a grown woman, brings Edgar Linton (whom in her superficial attraction for exactly this kind of luxury, she has married) the news of Heathcliff's return and asks if she is to bring him into the parlor, the appropriate setting of gentility, he looks "vexed" and suggests "the kitchen as a more suitable place" for him. By so doing he conforms to the nature of his own world, which has created an elaborate system of social distinctions to deaden the impact, at once vivifying and destructive, of essential passion; but Catherine, true to the promptings of her deeper nature, replies by instructing Nelly to prepare two tables, "one for your master and Miss Isabella being gentry; the other for Heathcliff and myself, being of the lower orders." To the social distinction thus stressed by the Lintons as human, civilizing, and repudiated as irrelevant, life-denying by Catherine, correspond a number of findings in the moral order which belong to the book's very substance. The most significant of these throw an adverse light upon the Linton claim to superiority of character. "Pettish," "silly," "whining," "envious" are the adjectives applied to Edgar by Catherine; and Emily Brontë is at some pains to relate them to the world of pampered luxury in which the family are represented as living. It is no accident that the man who, as a child, had been protected by bull-dogs from the intrusion into the family property of two harmless children calls upon his servants, after attempting to retire himself, to eject his hated rival from his house. As we come to know the Lintons better,[4] we find beneath their richly and essentially unformed character refinement undoubtedly, but also selfishness, meanness, and even a cruelty which, although very different from Heathcliff's brutality, is hardly less inhuman in some of its manifestations.

---

[4] When Charlotte, in her Preface to the 1850 edition, singles out Edgar as "an example of constancy and tenderness," she is surely showing something less than a complete understanding of the nature of her sister's genius.

It is in part his reaction against the debased civilization represented by the Lintons that induces Heathcliff to embark upon the destructive activity which finally brings him to his death.

For it is, after all, destruction, a dedication to death, that results from Catherine's faith and Heathcliff's somber intensity. To see in *Wuthering Heights* no more than a plain contrast between civilized decadence and primitive vitality would, indeed, be too simple. Beneath Catherine's love for Heathcliff lies a genuine conflict, a clash of different levels of passion which ends by consuming her. The part of her nature which craves civilized, social fulfilment is sufficiently attracted by the agreeable aspects of life in the society of the Lintons to marry Edgar and become part of the family. She herself never refuses the name of "love" to her feeling for Edgar. Yet this love—and here we return to the deeper content of the novel, its exploration of the conflicting depths of personality—can satisfy only the more superficial part of her nature. All that is most powerful and permanent in her repudiates Linton, impels her to return to Heathcliff; through the whole of her story we are faced with the contrast between the "foliage" which changes and the "eternal rocks" beneath. Yet the foliage, though in no sense fundamental, represents a reality, even—on its own level—a necessity, which cannot be ignored without simplifying unduly the profound balance of conflicting sensations upon which the novel rests.

Wuthering Heights represents, in other words, not the statement of a "naturalist" thesis, or a return to primitive instinct, but a genuine clash of emotional states; and it is the clash, not the thesis, or even any attempt at resolution, that gives the novel its unique character and power. This clash, indeed, animates one of the most surprising and beautiful passages of the book. In it Cathy, daughter of Catherine and Edgar Linton, and thereby heiress to two conflicting outlooks, describes a discussion between herself and the sickly son of Heathcliff and Isabella Linton:

> "One time, however, we were near quarrelling. He said the pleasantest manner of spending a hot July day was lying from morning till evening on a bank of heath in the middle of the moors, with the bees humming dreamily about among the bloom, and the larks singing high up over head, and the blue sky and bright sun shining steadily and cloudlessly. That was his most perfect idea of heaven's happiness: mine was rocking in a rustling green tree, with a west wind blowing, and bright white clouds flitting rapidly above; and not only larks, but throstles, and blackbirds, and linnets, and cuckoos pouring out music on every side, and the moors seen at a

distance, broken into cool dusky dells; but close by great swells of long grass undulating in waves to the breeze; and woods and sounding water, and the whole world awake and wild with joy. He wanted all to lie in an ecstacy of peace; I wanted all to sparkle, and dance in a glorious jubilee. I said his heaven would be only half alive; and he said mine would be drunk: I said I should fall asleep in his; and he said he could not breathe in mine, and began to grow very snappish."

Here once more we may detect the intense operation of that peculiar spiritual emotion which Emily Brontë imparted to her characters. The emotion is of the same type as we find in the most personal of her poems. It is characteristic of the essentially religious nature of her inspiration that what begins as a discussion of the best way of passing a hot summer's day turns rapidly into a comparison between two contrasted ideas of the nature of celestial happiness. If Linton appears to be concerned with no more than "the *pleasantest* manner" of passing a July day, whereas Catherine begins by transforming "pleasant" into "perfect" and thereby shifts the conception of felicity to quite another level, the implied difference can be defined in strictly literary terms. It is underlined, above all, by the contrasted choice of adjectives in the two parts of the speech. For Linton the bees hum "dreamily," the sun shines "steadily" and "cloudlessly" in the sky; the ideal which attracts him, and which finds reflection even in the tranquil immobility of the prose rhythm in the parts of Cathy's speech which refer to him, is one of stillness, passivity, peace. It is only when she sets against it her own thirst for identification with a world in which vitality finds expression in an increasing emotional tempo that the tone of the speech is transformed: for she imagines herself "rocking" at the heart of a world in motion, with the wind "blowing" and the clouds "flitting rapidly above" and all this leads up to an overpowering vision of the birds —not of one kind alone, like Linton's larks invisibly suspended in the heights of a uniform blue sky, but innumerable and diversified in species—"pouring out music on every side," whilst the grass is "undulating" to the breeze, the water "sounding," and "the whole world *awake* and *wild* with joy."

What is at stake here, as well as two different reactions to natural beauty, is a clash between two opposed conceptions of life, each of which gives, by contrast, added meaning to its opposite. For Linton Heathcliff, life tends to peace, calm passivity; for Cathy, it consists in active identification with the surrounding world. Yet the fact that Cathy's emotion is so powerful as to sweep aside the impression of passivity left by Linton cannot alter the fact that both emotions formed a part of Emily Brontë's intuition of life, that Catherine's identification with the forces of universal motion tended as its end towards a peace and quiescence which, if not that of Linton, is none the less implied in the novel. That its authoress felt *both* emotions, that her own creative impulse rested upon the balance, the tension set up between them, is sufficiently clear from this passage and from others which abound in the book. If her characteristic reaction to nature was one of eager and active acceptance, it is also true that she sought through and beyond this acceptance an intuition of permanence which was essentially contemplative. The impulse to unite these two necessities of her nature is the true source of the inspiration of her novel.

This craving for unity expressed itself in *Wuthering Heights* through the stress repeatedly laid upon yet another element, itself romantic in origin, of the emotional make-up of the novel: the tendency to see human life and individual passions in the shadow of death. The presence of death is felt intensely in *Wuthering Heights*, at times as something against which the protagonists react with all the force of their passionate energies, and at times as a profoundly evocative intuition of peace. The two attitudes need to be seen in relation to one another if we are not to simplify excessively the true nature of the emotion which the novel conveys. The death of Mr. Earnshaw and the final lingering of the narrator over the graves of the sleepers "in that *quiet* earth," characteristic as they are of Emily Brontë, no doubt owe part of their inspiration to an attraction for the idea of peace through dissolution which can be associated with adolescent emotion. They do not, however, stand alone. For a proper estimate of their importance we need to recall other and closely associated phrases which point to emotions of a more complex kind. When Nelly Dean, after Mr. Earnshaw's death, hears the children comforting each other for their loss, she makes, indeed, her own sentimental comment—"no person in the world ever pictured heaven so beautifully as they did in their innocent talk"; but the comment is not the last word, and the next sentence comes as the intrusion of a more real and more truly tragic experience, as unexpected as it is profoundly moving in its simplicity: "While I sobbed and listened, I could not help wishing we were all there *safe* together." The end of Heathcliff, too, stands in the closest relation to a tragedy in which life and death, the exclusive fulfilment of passion and the self-destruction which inevitably accompanies it, are inextricably fused. If he appears at the end of the novel to have found a kind of peace in death, one of his last phrases recalls once more that his was no simple slipping into unconsciousness, no surrender to the craving for fictitious repose: "My soul's bliss kills my body, but does not satisfy itself." The phrase is Emily Brontë's, but the spirit of metaphysical passion which animates it, the consuming desire for a completeness unattainable in time but implied by temporal experience, is not—when due allowance has been made for the world of differences which separated her from Christian belief—altogether remote from that of religious experience.

Preface to *Wuthering Heights*

by Albert J. Guérard

A fine modern novelist, Mark Schorer, has praised *Wuthering Heights* as one of the most carefully constructed novels in the language, and various critics have pointed to its several symmetries of arrangement. This attitude toward the novel's form seems to me seriously open to question, however. I find instead a dark, splendid, imperfect novel that occasionally loses control of its major attitudes and emphases. But the theoretical conception governing its structure is clear enough. This is that the tragic story repeats itself, or threatens to, in the second generation, with each of the blind roles resumed by a new actor, and the old sufferings re-enacted. The first Cathy, Catherine Earnshaw, has enjoyed her rough-and-tumble childhood with the parentless Heathcliff, and is so deeply attached to him that he seems a very part of her being. But his native wildness, aggravated by Hindley Earnshaw's brutality, leaves him half-literate and uncouth, and Cathy chooses to marry the polished and effeminate Edgar Linton instead. She assumes, oddly enough, that she can maintain the two relationships, the social and the ungoverned, the married and the passionate, but this proves impossible. With the definitive splitting, the irreversible separation of Heathcliff and Edgar Linton, Catherine chooses to die. Heathcliff thereafter is devoted to two obsessional designs: he will revenge himself on life by forcing the next generation of Lintons and Earnshaws to re-enact this tragic story, and he will try to communicate with the dead Cathy for the seventeen remaining years of his life. Her death, it may be noted, occurs almost exactly in the middle of the book.

In the second half, the brutal role of Hindley is assumed by Heathcliff, who tries to degrade Hareton Earnshaw as he himself had been degraded. But the lovers of the second generation are weakened versions, parodies almost, of their predecessors. Linton

From sections II and III of Preface to Wuthering Heights, *by Albert J. Guérard. Copyright, 1960, by Washington Square Press, Inc. Reprinted by permission of Washington Square Press, Inc.*

Heathcliff is a grotesque candy-sucking replacement for Edgar
Linton, Hareton is a coarser but less aggressive Heathcliff, Cathy
Linton a sweeter but less vivacious Cathy Earnshaw. All this was, of
course, intended by the author, who may have had her theories of
heredity and degeneration. But it is not clear what these recurrences
accomplish, except to illustrate Heathcliff's inhumanity. It is perhaps suggested that a diabolic savage force has been controlled and
domesticated, thus making a happy marriage at last possible. Yet
many readers must feel rather the tragic loss of primitive force and
energy; this small world has weakened. And so too have the author's
energy of phrasing and power to dramatize scenes; the writing has
become listless. Only the audacious final pages of Heathcliff's des-
perate attempt to communicate with Cathy's ghost show some of
the earlier strength. Then abruptly we recover much of the sympathy
we felt for him, over three hundred pages earlier, when he burst into
tears and (overheard by the irritatingly obtuse Lockwood) made his
moving appeal: "Come in! come in!" he sobbed. "Cathy, do come.
Oh do—*once* more! Oh! my heart's darling; hear me *this* time—
Catherine, at last!"

It is precisely here—in the very fact that over three hundred pages
separate the two appeals—that the most disturbing structural weakness lies. For it determines the novel's erratic and uncertain treatment of Heathcliff. The possibility existed for just such a complex
view, minutely balancing rational judgment and sympathy, as Conrad would take of Lord Jim or Faulkner of Thomas Sutpen. There
is rich ambiguity even in the account of Heathcliff's coming, in the
mystery of his origin. Is he homeless waif to be pitied or diabolic
emissary to be feared? The effeminate, blundering intrusions of
Lockwood increase our sympathy for Heathcliff in the opening
pages; so too, later, does the shrill excessive "demonizing" of Nelly,
who is in this comparable to Faulkner's Miss Rosa. And from the
vantage of the final pages we may see, at last, the two Heathcliffs
juxtaposed, each demanding some response: the faithful, tormented
lover attempting over all the years to communicate with his dead
Cathy and the brutal even sadistic husband, father and head of
household. But this juxtaposition cannot be made from a reading of
the middle portion of the novel. It cannot be experienced; it can
only be reconstructed. For we are allowed to forget too long that
one fidelity and redeeming obsession. Was the radical incompleteness
of the portrait in the middle section deliberate or inadvertent? It is
perhaps impossible to know. But there are many signs to suggest not
a controlled manipulation of the reader's view of Heathcliff, but,

rather, violent oscillations of the author's. In dramatizing the brute, she too may have forgotten the sufferer.

The novel survives, however, this imbalance and uncertainty. It may be asked where in *Wuthering Heights* lies that particular vision of things and fundamental human truth that most great novels possess—the controlling preoccupation or obsession, perhaps unemphasized and even unintended by its author, living it may be a secret life beneath the surface of the story, yet intensifying and enriching that surface? The word *theme* seems too crude for what may often be, rather, a significant strangeness, an *illuminating distortion* and hidden source of creative energy. It is, in one sense, the novel's true center. Some readers might find it in Heathcliff's "grand passion" and fidelity that make all else, even goodness, seem irrelevant. This is a human concern fundamental enough, here enriched by a macabre fantasy of total communication with the loved one even beyond the grave, even at last within it. Or the illuminating distortion might lie in the queer pattern of re-enactment, so savagely encouraged by Heathcliff. Or it might lie in an overriding impression of sexual puissance: Heathcliff the diabolic who yet represents primordial energies, surrounded by enfeebled or impotent lovers. According to Mark Schorer, the novel's unintended meaning, discovered by its technique, lies in its "devastating spectacle of human waste," the ruin of unmoral passion.

All this may be true. Doubtless only a woman could have imagined such a figure of masculine power—insubordinate and vindictive and faithful—to be subdued and domesticated only by proxy, in the personage of Hareton Earnshaw. But it is also natural to look for some illuminating distortion in the elder Cathy, with whom Emily Brontë so identified. Here the central oddity—and for me it seems the major one of *Wuthering Heights*—lies in Cathy's attitude toward Heathcliff and Edgar Linton, as expressed both on the evening of her engagement to Edgar and in her behavior after Heathcliff returns. The oddity is that Cathy expects to "have them both," finds this expectation entirely "natural," and is enraged because neither Heathcliff nor Edgar will consent to such a *ménage-à-trois*.

The first crucial scene is awkward enough, as scenes often are which bear an intolerable or censorable meaning and burden. The chance of an injury had exposed Cathy to the amusing, flattering, civilized society of Thrushcross Grange, and to the refined Edgar Linton. Thereafter, she adopts a "double character without exactly intending to deceive any one"; she hides her "rough side" when with

the Lintons, but indulges it with Heathcliff. The issue is drawn in
Chapter IX. She consents to marry Edgar because he is handsome,
young, cheerful, pleasant, loving, rich. But her answer—when Nelly
asks her how Heathcliff will bear this separation—is explosive:

> "He quite deserted! we separated!" she exclaimed, with an accent
> of indignation. "Who is to separate us, pray? They'll meet the fate
> of Milo! Not as long as I live, Ellen—for no mortal creature. Every
> Linton on the face of the earth might melt into nothing, before I
> could consent to forsake Heathcliff. Oh, that's not what I intend—
> that's not what I mean! I shouldn't be Mrs. Linton were such a price
> demanded! He'll be as much to me as he has been all his lifetime.
> Edgar must shake off his antipathy, and tolerate him, at least."

She goes on to reason, less persuasively, that by marrying Linton
she can help Heathcliff rise. Her truer response was that initial and
instinctive one; that of course she may have the two lovers. And
now she returns to that queer area of speculation, and moves toward
the novel's most famous sentence:

> ". . . I cannot express it; but surely you and everybody have a notion
> that there is, or should be an existence of yours beyond you. What
> were the use of my creation if I were entirely contained here? My
> great miseries in this world have been Heathcliff's miseries, and I
> watched and felt each from the beginning; my great thought in
> living is himself. If all else perished, and *he* remained, I should
> still continue to be; and if all else remained, and he were annihilated,
> the universe would turn to a mighty stranger. I should not seem a
> part of it. My love for Linton is like the foliage in the woods. Time
> will change it, I'm well aware, as winter changes the trees. My love
> for Heathcliff resembles the eternal rocks beneath—a source of little
> visible delight, but necessary. Nelly, I *am* Heathcliff—he's always,
> always in my mind—not as a pleasure, any more than I am always a
> pleasure to myself—but as my own being—so don't talk of our sep-
> aration again—it is impracticable. . . ."

How "impracticable" the separation must be we learn in the
eleventh and twelfth chapters. Cathy speaks of her "constant indulgence of one's weak nature, and the other's bad one." But neither
lover—the weak husband or the fiery, vengeful Heathcliff—will
accept a reconciliation, and Cathy simply elects to die. Her decision
seems absurd, at first, since it appears to be largely grounded in
nervous irritation and pique. But in some very real sense the decision is thrust upon her, and for deeper reasons: she *cannot* live unless she possesses both men, the two reconciled as it were within her.
What does this fantasy mean, and what is the particular place of

Heathcliff in this triad? In a quite open and innocuous sense (innocuous at least to the normal Victorian reader) Heathcliff is an infantile attachment, the childhood companion associated with the old lost freedom of the fields. The two children grew up "rude as savages," and "in absolute heathenism." Later, in the hour of her suicidal exposure to the icy air, Cathy longs for that old freedom: "I wish I were a girl again, half savage and hardy, and free; and laughing at injuries, not maddening under them!"

Less openly, but with greater force, the issue is social and sexual. This is true even though, presumably, no sexual acts ouside marriage occur. Both Cathy and Heathcliff (whose own masculine energy is unmistakable) insist on Edgar Linton's weakness; so too does the novel's recurring emphasis on windows and locked doors and keys, and on the resonances of fire and ice. Duty, humanity, pity, charity —these are what Edgar has to offer the restless and dying Cathy. "He might as well plant an oak in a flowerpot, and expect it to thrive, as imagine he can restore her to vigour in the soil of his shallow cares!" And yet Cathy had loved Edgar Linton and wanted to marry him. Her not unreasonable longing was to have both Edgar's tender and intelligent companionship and Heathcliff's sexual energy. Her mistake of course was to recognize, in the place of such sexual energy, a nameless, free-floating and "permissible" passion. It is reasonable to suppose the author also saw, if dimly, the nature of the mistake. Emily Brontë conceived, sanely enough, a marriage combining sexuality and quiet affection, but could realize her conception only in the attenuated flesh and spirit of Hareton Earnshaw, that domesticated savage who learns to read.

The terms of the oddity, of the illuminating distortion, are inevitably larger than these, until they do indeed achieve a fundamental truth. For what the novel also imagines, at this moment when both Edgar Linton and Heathcliff must be retained, is no less than a reconciliation of our profoundest antinomies of spirit and most opposed modes of being: on the one hand the social, ethical, conscious, rational, institutional (with all the comforts these bring) and on the other individual, free, irrational, unconscious, atavistic (with all the life energies these signify). This is a reconciliation within the personality, but has its bearing on social behavior. That other reconciliation society commends, and indeed commands, is a taming rather than a balancing; victory, not coexistence. This is what the last pages of *Wuthering Heights* also commend in a wholly conscious, doubtless intelligent way. Education and society triumph; primitive energies are leashed, very nearly annulled. But in the novel's most vital pages the dream is truly that of a happy co-existence—less harmony than coexistence—in which nothing is lost. The pleasures of control and reason are enjoyed. But the outlaw and unconscious self is nevertheless left free, still insubordinate, un-damaged and alive.

The Circumambient Universe

by J. Frank Goodridge

The Two Houses

Wuthering Heights gains universality by the special values it gives
to every feature in a remote, provincial setting; and its chief features
are the two rival houses which are always in the foreground. In other
novels whose titles are the names of houses (*Mansfield Park, Bleak
House, Howards End*) those houses represent certain traditional
values to which all their events are to be in some way referred.
Though the Heights, considered as the family home of the Earnshaws, has something of this symbolic function, under Heathcliff's
domination it becomes much more. It seems to be the home of all
those natural forces, death-dealing or life-giving, which it is built
to withstand; the fate of the Lintons, as well as the Earnshaws, depends on their relationship to it.

Lockwood explains the meaning of its name: "a significant
provincial adjective, descriptive of *the atmospheric tumult to which
its station is exposed in stormy weather.*" [1] It is clearly no Castle of
Otranto. Brontë takes pains to stress its ordinariness, its rude,
provincial homeliness. But its chief characteristics are exposure to
the power of the wind, and fortress-like strength.

Much is made in *Wuthering Heights* of this contrast between
exposure and enclosure, the world within and the world outside, suggested by Lockwood's opening description. A great deal of the action
has to do with doors and windows (whether open or closed) and

---

From Emily Brontë: Wuthering Heights, *Chapter II, "The Circumambient
Universe" (London, Edward Arnold, Ltd., 1964). Copyright 1964 by J. F. Goodridge. Reprinted by permission of Edward Arnold, Ltd.*

[1] Wuther or Whither (O.N.), *dial.*, to move swiftly with force; to make a
sullen roaring, as the wind; to throw or beat violently (*Chambers Twentieth
Century Dictionary*). It is natural to associate this with the English verbs
"weather" and "wither," which suggest both the destructive and the restorative
effects of wind and sunshine.

the crossing of thresholds (going out or coming in). The Heights seems to depend for its survival on its isolation from the world beyond the moor: and all the main sources of conflict (Heathcliff, Frances, and the foreign luxuries of the Grange) originate from outside.

As the protagonists are repeatedly subjected to rain, wind and sun, the theme of exposure to the elements gains in depth and complexity throughout the novel. The tumult of the elements is associated with the tumult of supernatural forces which Heathcliff and Catherine are not afraid of. "These spiritual powers," writes Mr. J. Hillis Miller, "are immanent in nature, and identified with its secret life. The expression of this double life in *Wuthering Heights,* as in Emily Brontë's poems, is an ancient and primitive symbol: the wind." [2] We should consider, too, how throughout the novel human beings are described, especially by Catherine and Heathcliff, in animal images, which Brontë uses as emblems of the breaking down of barriers between the animal and the human.

On the Heights, the effects of weather are unsoftened. At Thrushcross Grange they are always gentler, filtered and diluted. Heathcliff and Catherine, brought up in the wild exposure of the Heights, are deprived of all civilized comforts. But the Grange is a house of soft, clinging luxury whose inmates are guarded by servants and bulldogs. For Cathy it is a walled Eden, with Heathcliff a Satan tempting her from without. The typical view from the Grange is through an open, first-floor lattice, from which Catherine looks beyond the walled gardens and courts into the idyllic glen with its murmuring beck, and on to the kirk and moor beyond, which hides "Wuthering Heights" from sight. Thus the world outside is framed like a picture, and it is only when the story is set at the Grange that we are conscious of nature as a background, at one remove from human lives.

In Jane Austen's *Sense and Responsibility,* Marianne Dashwood's habit of taking solitary walks round the grounds of Cleveland is satirized as a self-conscious affectation, and her imprudence in getting her feet wet is punished by a serious illness. When Catherine exposes herself to the thunderstorm and sits all night on the settle in her wet clothes, she too is reproved by Nelly for her folly. But Nelly's common sense is often shown to be inadequate: it does not stand, like Jane Austen's, between actions and our judgment of

---

[2] *The Disappearance of God.* An examination of the use Brontë makes of images of light and darkness (especially the association of dusk with the supernatural, and the contrast between natural and artificial light—the candles of the Heights and glimmering tapers of the Grange) is equally suggestive.

them (notice in this case Catherine's answers to Hindley's questions). Jane Austen was concerned to uphold the fabric of civilized society, while Brontë simply shows us what life is like both with, and without, civilized refinements—close to nature, or cut off from it.

Given the conditions, we are convinced of the truth of Catherine's passion: her despair over the loss of Heathcliff weighs more heavily on her than her drenched garments. As often in *Wuthering Heights,* there is here a genuine interaction between human passion and natural phenomena. An uncontrollable passion draws her out of the defenses of the house into the storm; the storm in turn drenches her to the skin and she brings its effects back into the house.

The elements of nature in *Wuthering Heights* are not merely symbols. The rain is the rain, and the sun the sun. The moor which is Catherine's heaven is not the symbol of her love for Heathcliff. Her love is the bedrock of her life, because with him she had experienced the wild, free life of the moor, and he shared its character: "An unreclaimed creature, without refinement, without cultivation: an arid wilderness of furze and whinstone."

The exposed wilderness of unreclaimed nature is, for Brontë, the rock beneath the cultivated soil of human life, from which all our passions are ultimately derived. The two houses show us two possible ways of living: the one rock-like, built on the Heights, a bastion against the weather yet perilously close to the wild elements; the other crouched in the cultivated valley and standing in a sheltered park.

The Heights is a functional house: we are made aware of its architectural structure, within and without. Its roof "had never been underdrawn: Its entire anatomy lay bare to an enquiring eye." (I) But at no point are we given an architectural impression of the Grange. Instead, we look into its interior with Heathcliff and Catherine, and see it as "a splendid place," rich, carpeted and cushioned with crimson. Decorated with delicate ornamentation in gold and silver and lit with soft, artificial light, it belongs to a "civilisation" which values comfort more than life itself. Its children are spoiled and pampered so much that they are robbed of all connection with the sources of natural feeling.[3]

[3] Notice, in this connection, the important references to books and reading throughout the novel. For the children of the Heights, books provide an essential means of cultivation—Heathcliff's deterioration is largely due to his failure to "keep up an equality with Catherine in her studies . . . he yielded with poignant though silent regret . . . ," etc. But to those at the Grange, books only provide a means of escape: we associate them with heartlessness and lack of spirit (XII and elsewhere).

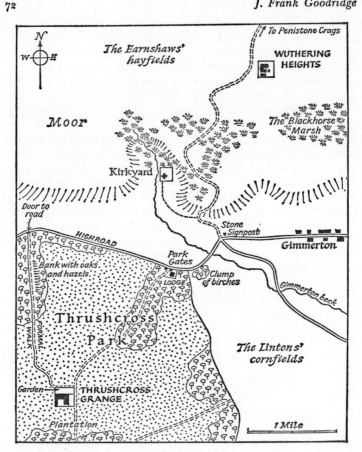

The Kirk

Apart from the two houses, there is one other important feature in Brontë's landscape—the kirk, sometimes referred to as Gimmerton "chapel." It stands about half-way between the two houses, on the edge of the moor. When Lockwood first introduces it to us in III, he describes its situation, close to a swamp which embalms the corpses in the churchyard, and tells us why, in 1801, it had no pastor.

Before the death of Frances, the Earnshaws had been regular churchgoers and the curate, Shielders, had educated their children.

Soon after her death, the curate stopped calling, and in XI the child Hareton tells Nelly: "I was told the curate should have his —— teeth dashed down his —— throat, if he stepped over the threshold. . . ." The Lintons also had attended church; but after Catherine's death, though Cathy went to the "chapel" occasionally, Edgar ceased to attend, for his grief transformed him "into a complete hermit" (XVII). He only visited the churchyard in order to lie on the green mound of Catherine's grave, on every anniversary of her death.

Thus the church itself diminishes in importance until, on his last visit, Lockwood finds it falling into decay. For Catherine, to the surprise of the villagers, had chosen to be buried, not in the chapel, under the carved monuments of the Lintons, but "on a green slope in the corner of the kirkyard, where the wall is so low that heath and bilberry plants have climbed over it from the moor; and the peat-mould almost buries it" (XVI). So for Edgar and Heathcliff, the masters of the two houses, this grave takes the place of the kirk as a center of devotion and the traditional Christianity of the parish, once common to the Lintons and the Earnshaws, is superseded.

Worlds of Heaven and Hell

What have those lonely mountains worth revealing?
More glory and more grief than I can tell:
The earth that wakes *one* human heart to feeling
Can centre both the worlds of Heaven and Hell.
Attributed to Emily Brontë[4]

It is useful in interpreting *Wuthering Heights* to consider the frequent use in it of the words "heaven" and "hell" and other terms of salvation and damnation. The ready-to-hand hyperbole of heaven and hell had been overworked, especially in love-poetry, before Brontë's time,[5] and only a handful of English poets and dramatists (Marlowe, Shakespeare, Milton and Blake among them) had ever added much to the imaginative impact of these words. But in *Dr. Faustus*[6] and *Paradise Lost*, for example, the words derive their force largely from the assumption that heaven and hell exist, as

[4] Hatfield (*Collected Poems of Emily Brontë*) thinks that this poem, "Often rebuked, yet always back returning," was written by Charlotte to express her thoughts about her sister.
[5] Cf., Scott's "Love is heaven, and heaven is love" in *The Lay of the Last Minstrel*.
[6] Cf., "Hell hath no limits, nor is circumscribed . . . ," etc. (*Dr. Faustus*, 560).

objective, theological facts. In Brontë, the theological facts appear to exist only as shadows of Victorian hypocrisy; the reality to which they refer varies from person to person. The novel's whole pattern is designed to convince us that Heathcliff is *not* talking nonsense when he says, speaking of his own burial: "No minister need come; nor need anything be said over me—I tell you I have nearly attained *my* heaven; and that of others is altogether unvalued and un-coveted by me."

Throughout the novel's intricate pattern, a number of private heavens and hells are contrasted, each throwing the others into sharper relief. They intersect one another at many points—the dis-torted "circles" of an Inferno-cum-Paradiso centred on Heathcliff and Catherine.

There is, first, Lockwood's "perfect misanthropist's heaven." On his final visit to the Heights, this landscape (which he has not seen before in summer) does indeed appear, as he puts it, "divine." It is transfigured by the love of Cathy and Hareton, and he now looks upon their romance with a pang of envy. Since he has not himself experienced the "purgatory" of the Heights at first hand, as Cathy has, it is a "heaven" in which he can have no permanent place.

Brontë uses the Latinate "paradise," "elysium," etc., only for the comparatively trivial or selfish contentments of those who are in-capable of a greater happiness. So, for example, Hindley sits with Frances in his "paradise" by the hearth, while Heathcliff and Catherine create their own "heaven" together. We have noticed, too, that behind Nelly's religiosity there lies a fairy land of childhood which she passes on to Cathy through her "nursery lore"; and that from this Cathy creates the Wordsworthian "heaven" of her child-hood. This is directly contrasted with Linton's drowsy heaven, which is really "infantile" in the modern sense. Thus Cathy: " 'This is something like your paradise,' said she, making an effort at cheer-fulness,"—and a few minutes later, " 'I can't tell why we should stay. He's asleep. . . .' " (XXVI)

Joseph's private heaven in the kitchen, far more solid and in-destructible, is described in this way: "Joseph seemed sitting in a sort of elysium alone, beside a roaring fire; a quart of ale on the table near him, bristling with large pieces of toasted oat-cake; and his black, short pipe in his mouth." Since first exiled from the family sitting-room after Mr. Earnshaw's death, he has refused to admit that the Heights affords any civilized comforts other than the kitchen with its porridge, and the garrets with their sacks of malt and grain —the coarse essentials of life which he shares with Hareton:

" *'Parlour!'* he echoed sneeringly, *'parlour!* Nay, we've noa *parlours.
. . .'* " (XIII—Isabella's letter provides the best material for the study of Joseph.)

Though originally a usurper, Joseph grows in stature, becoming the upholder of the old Earnshaw tradition—his rough oatmeal-hospitality opposed to all refinements. He instils into Hareton a pride of name and lineage (XVII), and though driven in the end from his own "hearthstun," he is reinstated at last as Hareton's tenant, as if in recognition of his strength and persistence. We see his tenacity most clearly in Isabella's narrative (XVII). Heathcliff pushes him on to his knees to mop up Hindley's blood, he joins his hands, begins to pray and then rises, vowing he will go to the Grange at once to fetch Mr. Linton, the magistrate. So obstinate is his defiance of Heathcliff, that his master is forced on to the defensive. Thus his "elysium," though selfish, is not represented to us as wholly unscrupulous. It is a way of life fit to survive (Joseph keeps the farmwork going); and the Heights without Joseph would scarcely live in our imagination as a real household.

For Isabella, on the other hand, the Heights proves a sterile "purgatory" inciting her only to hatred. But to Cathy it is a fruitful one, making possible her love for Hareton. For Hindley, too, the Heights becomes a real hell. Deprived of Frances, and having no better religion than Joseph's to support him, he falls into frenzied despair: "He neither wept nor prayed; he cursed and defied: execrated God and man, and gave himself up to reckless dissipation" (VIII). His speeches are filled with the language of perdition.

Hindley's conventional form of despair is deliberately set against Edgar's equally conventional expressions of hope and trust in God's providence. Nelly, who speaks for Edgar in matters of religious sentiment, makes this contrast explicit: "I used to draw a comparison between him and Hindley. . . . One hoped, and the other despaired: they chose their lots, and were righteously doomed to endure them. . . ." This complacently homiletic language suits them both; for Hindley's curses only reveal his helplessness, while Edgar's sanctity (he dies blissfully, like a saint) is as ineffectual as Hindley's blasphemy. Both lose all they possess to the wiles of Heathcliff.

The Peat-mould

No more need be said here of the heavens and hells of Catherine and Heathcliff, since this commentary has been largely concerned with them. Lying in the peat-mould after her death, Catherine exercises a greater power than she did in life. As the story progresses, Edgar's thoughts, no less than Heathcliff's, become centred on the kirkyard. His longing to share her death (in a sense, he is ahead of Heathcliff in this) easily takes away the importance for him of his social functions as a landed gentleman, a magistrate and a parish-ioner of Gimmerton. Catherine's spirit, still alive in the earth and on the Heights, draws first Edgar, then Heathcliff, into its own "heaven," which belongs to the world of nature, above and beyond the kirk: "It's a rough journey, and a sad heart to travel it; and we must pass by Gimmerton Kirk, to go that journey! We've braved its ghosts often together, and dared each other to stand among the graves and ask them to come. But, Heathcliff, if I dare you now, will you venture? If you do, I'll keep you. I'll not lie there by myself: they may bury me twelve feet deep, and throw the church down over me, but I won't rest till you are with me. I never will!"

So Catherine's "green slope," where Lockwood stands at the end of the novel, is a symbol of the final harmony which Nature's economy has woven out of the conflicting heavens and hells. In the decay of the kirk itself, we see the decay of Victorian Christianity. And the grave "half buried beneath the heath," where Catherine lies at peace between Edgar and Heathcliff, is the sign that her re-bellion against God's providence has triumphed at last: she has passed by Gimmerton Kirk, and found again, with Heathcliff, her "heaven" in the middle of the moor.

An Absolute Hierarchy

Nature is thus seen in the novel as a complex of spiritual forces, embodying all that can be apprehended of fate and the supernatural. Its workings are beyond good and evil in the social and moral sense. Only that which is strong and instinct with passionate feeling sur-vives: Brontë's nature has no place for cold-hearted sentiment, soft-ness, kindly religiosity or conventional moralism.

The setting of the novel is such that lawlessness and superstition lie close to the edge of an imperilled civilization, where two de-caying religious traditions, one sentimentally pietistic, the other crudely Calvinistic, give rise to the dominant images of Heaven and Hell. The traditional, biblical language is caught up in a drama of violent passion and pre-Christian belief, which carries it very far from its original moorings. In place of a traditional Christianity and its social values, different forms of animism—savagely heathen or limpidly Wordsworthian—spring to life, passions of love and venge-ance being expressed in a language that is partly a revivification of the old religious jargons, and partly that of a newly-animated nature-worship.

Yet in *Wuthering Heights,* human passions are always seen as co-existing with their opposites: the dictates of a homely common sense surround every outburst of feeling; and love, which gives rise to hatred and cruelty, triumphs in a story which lacks the element of Rousseau-like sentiment, and whose circumstances preclude affectation.

Brontë may lead us to question whether there is any one natural and social order, the same for all men and women. The conflicting individual heavens and hells confront one another at every turn: incompatible ways of life, coupled in grotesque ways sometimes lead to violence and hysteria, sometimes to lifeless neutrality and sometimes to new and fuller forms of life. Yet the novel is instinct with a sense of life's intensity and resilience, even defiance, in the face of misery and death. It makes no exclusive moral judgments, except, perhaps, one of hostility towards all complacent assumptions and artificial schemes of salvation. It leaves us with a host of unanswered questions and embodies no consistent philosophy of life. But its perfection of form is such that every event seems inevitable, and its subjective heavens and hells are raised to a level of universality.

Story and History in *Wuthering Heights*

by *Thomas A. Vogler*

After 120 years of reaction and explication, there is still no basic core of agreement on how *Wuthering Heights* is structured or what it is about. It has gone through several phases, corresponding rather closely to the changes in sensibility of its readers, but there has been no progressive exploration or accumulation of insight. From the earliest reactions, that this was a powerful but morbid novel of violent sexuality, there was a move to a purified view of the novel, an interpretation of Heathcliff and Catherine as sexless embodiments of the forces in an elemental dialectic. In the last few years, it has again become a sinister work, exhibiting the themes of incest, child violence, villainy, and authorial irony. Its structure was considered chaotic and confusing until C. P. Sanger's influential article revealed a detailed chronological pattern, after which it became a superbly structured novel. But again of late there has been a change; the pleasures of symmetry have waned, and fault is being found with the conclusion, which is seen as a weak and forced repetition of the first half.[1] It is not startling to discover that different and contradictory interpretations of the same work are generated endlessly by readers with different views of life and art. But it is distressing to realize that there is no context for the disagreements, no basic grasp of the elements or dynamics of fictional narrative, or of the problems inherent in the narrative form itself. As in too many other works, there is no openness to the novel, no recognition of the many clues and hints by which it tries to define its own mode of being. As long as *Wuthering Heights* is interpreted without taking stock of the problems and evaluations already incorporated in it by the author, our approach to it will be a quest for plot or for meaning which will be only a dim reflection of the furniture of our own brains. We shall find ourselves trapped like Isabella in her first impression of Heathcliff:

[1] The Sanger article is reprinted in this volume on page 15; the other views I mention are represented in the other selections.

"She abandoned them under a delusion," he answered; "picturing in me a hero of romance, and expecting unlimited indulgences from my chivalrous devotion. I can hardly regard her in the light of a rational creature, so obstinately has she persisted in forming a fabulous notion of my character, and acting on the false impressions she cherished."

In what follows, I propose to attempt to look at the novel with new eyes, and with as few preconceptions as possible. My hope is to follow some of the book's own clues towards what, in a neutral sense, I shall call its "structure."

There are two aspects of the book's beginning that deserve our attention. We are asked to read what follows as if it were a personal diary—dated, cut-off, private, and therefore close to the way Lockwood might speak to himself. This becomes even more important later, when we see that almost all of the important events, even though they are reported by Nelly Dean, are given in the words and personal voice of the participants. The other point to be noted is that the book begins with a problem of seeing. Lockwood enters the Heights with "an enquiring eye," alert to his surroundings and desiring to comprehend them in his own terms. We form an impression of what he expects to see as he enters, "inspecting the penetralium," and we observe his shocked surprise as he is disillusioned. Where he expects to find a "capital fellow," happily ensconced in a "perfect misanthropist's Heaven," he finds Heathcliff, a "singular contrast to his abode and style of living." Instead of a "canine mother," and dogs kept for pets, he finds "possessed swine . . . a brood of tigers." Instead of a cushion full of cats, he finds "Unluckily . . . a heap of dead rabbits." What we see in this is an idle, civilized, literary person, with preconceived notions of country life, and of life in general, being exposed to real people and forced to react. His reaction is to move from one preconceived, literary-based view to an opposite but equally removed view. From pampered pets to vicious beasts, from happy farmers to "wretched inmates" and "surly indigenae."

Lockwood feels unlucky in not finding things as he expected, as if it were a matter of chance. Heathcliff labels him "unhappy" in his "conjectures." It is clear that Lockwood is not finding a meaningful way to see the Heights or a way to fit in and be comfortable there. He is "laughing internally," thinking himself infinitely more "sociable" than his host. He is criticizing the inhabitants of the Heights for being cut off from their "species," but his own self-induced isolation is more immediately visible to the reader. Lockwood suggests this himself, when he describes his encounter at the sea coast with a "real goddess in my eyes," who becomes a "poor innocent" after further experience. The shift in this anecdote *("real goddess in my eyes"* to "poor innocent") parallels the shift we see in the beginning of the novel: from one extreme of preconceived vision to an opposite, presumably derived from the facts and therefore valid. Lockwood is able to see his own errors in the first instance ("No, I'm running on too fast—I bestow my own attributes too liberally on him"), and we agree with him, but whether or not we follow him in his process of revision and accept his final view is up to us.

At the beginning of the second chapter, we find that Lockwood has stationed himself in the Grange, that he sees Nelly Dean as "a matronly lady taken as a fixture along with the house," like the *ficelle* in a conventional novel. Lockwood is inclined to stay indoors by his study fire, and his chosen station at the Grange is clearly opposed to the "atmospheric tumult" of the Heights in almost every respect. In spite of his preference for the Grange, there are strong intimations that something there is wrong: his meal schedule cannot be met, there are no people (only fixtures), and the fire in his study is out. Since the facts of his environment have not met his demands or expectations, he retreats, walking the four miles to the Heights. When he gets there he is delighted to find what he missed at the Grange, a "huge, warm, cheerful apartment" with "an immense fire, compounded of coal, peat, and wood; and near the table, laid for a plentiful evening meal." There is thus something more elemental about Lockwood's second trip to the Heights, some dissatisfaction with his own state which he hopes to remedy. His questions this time are more open and direct, as if he hoped to find a more comprehensible form for the experiences that puzzled him on his first visit. He makes efforts to be sociable, by his own snobbish standards, with the selfish hope that if he handles them properly they will be what he desires as companions. But again he blunders. He takes Catherine for Heathcliff's "amiable lady," and is corrected: "Mrs. Heathcliff is my daughter-in-law." He takes Hareton for Cathy's husband, and is corrected: "My name is Hareton Earnshaw." The mistakes are in a sense reasonable, and the second is in fact prophetic; but there is something basically wrong which is reflected in Lockwood's diction. He expects (and wants) people to behave as they do in novels; he wants life to imitate a certain kind of art in the way in which life often does when people follow conventional roles in order to structure their experience. But these are people who do not choose to behave that way, and Lockwood is as helpless and lost as the reader expecting a conventional literary experience. Life is still imitating art, and art life, but Lockwood's conceptions are here shown to be included in, but not coterminous with, *Wuthering Heights.*

Thus his words reflect neither what is truly going on in his own mind, nor what is before him in the Heights; they are a game, disguise, and retreat for him, an anticipation in conversation of what he is doing in the composition of his diary. They are an attempt to cope with his experience in a way that will be palatable, rather than a way of communicating or discovering what is truly happening. His is a language which avoids violence by euphemism and inflates feebleness by exaggeration. As an extreme of artificial speech, contrasted with Heathcliff's raw, uncontrolled vehemence, it suggests at the very beginning the limitations of an isolated, literary point of view, and the very limits of language itself. It anticipates the opposite reaction of Heathcliff, in his most intense moment of experience ("Oh, God! it is unutterable."), and Heathcliff's reaction to Lockwood's "explanation" in Chapter III ("—God! he's mad to speak so!").

Yet in spite of, or even in part because of its artificiality, Lockwood's view does have some power over the reader's general impression of the Heights. Many readers view the Heights as a cruel, savage, inhospitable, other-worldly place simply because he gives them the words that fit that kind of place. Therefore, it is worth looking for a moment at the Heights through our own eyes, if only to correct Lockwood's over-reaction. If we do so, we see a place full of the sounds and smells of cooking, and the glow of a large fire. Animals are not kept as pets but their needs are respected.[2] We see Joseph "bringing in a pail of porridge for the dogs," and Hareton cannot be spared to guide Lockwood home, for "Who is to look after the horses, eh?" There are dead rabbits on a cushion, but the liver-colored bitch is "surrounded by a swarm of squealing puppies," and new life is very definitely going on. Lockwood is not received with his kind of hospitality, but he is invited in, offered wine, and his health is pledged. Lockwood assumes these are "prudential considerations of the folly of offending a good tenant," but this tells us more about his motivation than Heathcliff's. Hareton does offer,

[2] In contrast with the more "civilized" Grange, where the Linton children fight over the lap dog, nearly pulling it in two, and we see in Skulker a truly vicious dog, "his huge, purple tongue hanging half a foot out of his mouth, and his pendant lips streaming with bloody slaver." (Chapter VI.)

even after being insulted, to guide Lockwood part of the way home.
Catherine suggests that a man's life is of more consequence than
the animals'. It is quite possible to see the Heights as a microcosmic
world organized around a primitive but very basic concept of life.
There are no refinements, no civilized touches, but there are no
false idols either; and there is a genuine respect for the physical
order of being. One of the many paradoxes in the novel is how
Catherine and Heathcliff's spirituality is generated out of this re-
markably physical world, and how thoroughly marked by ma-
terialism and selfish possessiveness the inhabitants of the Grange
become.

The closer we look at Lockwood, the more he stands out as the
most violent and destructive element in this world of the Heights.
From the beginning, his horse's breast is "fairly pushing the barrier."
It is his "winking and making faces" at the dogs ("imagining they
would scarcely understand tacit insults") that causes their attack.
On his second visit he is downright violent, beating on the door
with hatred ("I will get in!"), staring hard at Cathy's "admirable
little form" on the sly, rudely ignoring Hareton's presence for five
minutes. His first thought after the misconception that Cathy is
Hareton's wife is both egotistic and malicious ("I must beware how
I cause her to regret her choice"), and he is hard put to resist box-
ing Hareton's ears (thinking him a servant) or to laugh out loud
at him. He takes Joseph's insult to Cathy as directed at himself, and
"sufficiently enraged, stepped towards the aged rascal with an intention of kicking him out of the door." He finally grabs the lantern
in a violent rage, and tries to fight his way out with it, only to be
stopped by the dogs and reduced to "several incoherent threats of
retaliation that, in their indefinite depths of virulency, smacked
of King Lear." The reference to Lear reflects his literary penchant
in a ridiculously grandiose moment. Lockwood is not a wronged
king, cruelly mistreated. He is not anything like the stuff Lears are
made from. But he is like Lear in being on the brink of a self-dis-
covery made possible by the loss of a world of appearances, and
the discovery of natural forces that cannot be denied. His mental
state even approaches Lear's madness; he is sick, dizzy and faint,
and he has grown progressively violent and incoherent in a context
which strongly suggests a regressive movement. Zillah appears at
the height of this movement in the role of a mother, to protect and
condole him, give him brandy and put him to bed. In the space of
a very few pages, Lockwood has been pushed to the edge of total
disorientation, his preconceived views shattered, and repressed im-

pulses released. When he finally escapes to return to the Grange at
the end of Chapter III, he must cross the blank stretches of snow,
making the two mile journey into four with his uncertain wonder-
ings:

> . . . the whole hill-back was one billowy, white ocean; the swells and
> falls not indicating corresponding rises and depressions in the ground
> —many pits, at least, were filled to a level; and entire ranges of
> mounds, the refuse of the quarries, blotted out from the chart which
> my yesterday's walk left pictured in my mind.

It is at that point that he turns to Nelly Dean's help to make
sense of his experience in the Heights. He turns the narrative over
to her, except for brief interruptions, for the remainder of the
novel. Her story is as much a ministry to him in his condition as
the hot gruel she brings while he crouches near the fire:

> . . . my head felt hot, and the rest of me chill; moreover, I was ex-
> cited, almost to a pitch of foolishness through my nerves and brain.
> This caused me to feel, not uncomfortable, but rather fearful, as I am
> still, of serious effects from the incidents of today and yesterday.

Nelly's authority to tell the story is that she has known and
experienced it all and can tell it as history. Before she begins to
fulfill her promise to tell "all about it," however, another mind has
entered the novel with its own story to live and tell. For the notes
of Catherine, scrawled on that "awful Sunday" when she and
Heathcliff decided to rebel, are no less than the beginning of a
different version—not different in fact, but totally different in structure and mode of perception.

The relationship between this story and that which Lockwood
is reporting is like that between the printed text of Catherine's
mildewed Testament and the "unformed, childish hand" which
scrawled the now "faded hieroglyphics," in a "not altogether . . .
legitimate purpose." Her method of writing violates the conventional
integrity of the printed Testament, making it more truly fit the
title she gives it ("Catherine Earnshaw, her book") and reflecting
the decision "to rebel" which is the substance of her message. She
writes for twenty minutes before the "scamper on the moor" which
we later learn took her and Heathcliff to the Grange. We must
now look at this small passage as an incipient story, comparable to
Lockwood's own journal, if we are to understand the further
development of Emily Brontë's novel which contains both.

Even though partly in "the form of a regular diary," like Lockwood's narrative, it is different from his in several crucial respects. It is recorded experience almost without context, written the moment after it happened. Although written "some quarter of a century back," it has a timeless vitality which causes us to connect it immediately to the other part of that Sunday's activities reported by Heathcliff when he returned to the Heights without Catherine. The spirit of rebellion she reports seems still in the air, still vibrant as Catherine is for Heathcliff even after her death. What is rejected, both in her rebellion and her reporting of it, is the whole frame of mind Lockwood and Nelly bring to the same history.

Perhaps the clearest place to see Nelly and Lockwood shaping the story together is at the end of Chapter VII. There Nelly points out that it is eleven o'clock, and perhaps time to stop the story; Lockwood replies, not that he will break his schedule for the story, but that "One or two is early enough for a person who lies till ten." Nelly then proposes to "leap over some three years" in the telling of her narrative, and Lockwood refuses to accept the skip. The jump would break his "tiresomely active" concentration on the story, which he likens to watching a cat licking itself "so intently that puss's neglect of one ear would put you seriously out of temper." The story has its own logic and necessity, like the cat's activity; but Lockwood is appropriating the story, utilizing it and demanding that it must somehow fit his frame of mind. It is at this point that Nelly gives her other qualifications for telling the story to Lockwood:

> "I certainly esteem myself a steady, reasonable kind of body," she said: "not exactly from living among the hills, and seeing one set of faces, and one series of actions, from year's end to year's end; but I have undergone sharp discipline, which has taught me wisdom; and then, I have read more than you would fancy, Mr. Lockwood. You could not open a book in this library that I have not looked into, and got something out of also. . . ."
>
> "However, if I am to follow my story in true gossip's fashion, I had better go on; and instead of leaping three years, I will be content to pass to the next summer—the summer of 1778, that is, nearly twenty-three years ago."

As much as a "poor man's daughter" can, Nelly has joined the enlightened and literary society that Lockwood belongs to. She too is trapped in schedules and tangled in time, and will tell the story consecutively, piece-by-piece, ordered in time. It is this shaping of the story that C. P. Sanger examined so thoroughly in his famous article, and which has been taken since for the groundwork and frame of the novel itself.

There are other important features of the Nelly-Lockwood narrative. Although qualified to tell the story because she was there, she attempts the feat of telling it without becoming a part of it. She has worked hard and had little time for personal feelings, and certainly not for larks on the moors like Cathy and Heathcliff. Together Lockwood and Nelly represent a number of almost institutionalized conventions, both in art and life, which give them their sense of form as events laid out on a chronological line leading to stasis. This can be a simple but effective principle of order, but it has its problems when the goal to be achieved through the ordering is either an aesthetic experience or a felt sense of the reality of life.[3] This principle rejects *discontinuity* and *simultaneity* both, as elements of life/experience and of art/narration. Life, thought, art, must adhere to *sequential movement* if that is the basic sense of how our lives proceed. The attitude is to be found in some religious notions of man's relation to God, where the present moment, the present life, is minimized as only a step toward the future resolution. Any emphasis on the present as containing the possibility of knowledge or vision of God is error.[4] As history, the attitude seeks a record of actual events arranged in chronological order, rejecting other forms such as myths which simply report that certain events occurred, as in a dream, without special emphasis on chronological sequence. Although I have been laboring the time-emphasis of this diachronic view, it should by now be obvious that more than mere time is involved. The diachronic view sees life changing slowly over a period of time; whether it be progress towards a goal or slow decay, the end is a stasis. The attitude conditions the total sense of life and art, as can be seen in its rejection of dreams, of the lapses in consciousness in which they occur, of childhood and its cultural equivalent in primitivism, of myth and, finally, of poetry:

> He who, in an enlightened and literary society, aspires to be a great poet, must first become a little child. He must take to pieces the whole

[3] Thus parodies of the attitude are legion. Tristram Shandy, struggling to tell his "life" from the first second; or Sancho, trying to tell the "perfect" story but losing it all because he could not include all the details (*Don Quixote*, The First Part, Chapter XX).

[4] Wesley, for example, dismissed all such attempts as "enthusiasm": "Trust not in visions or dreams; in sudden impressions, or strong impulses of any kind." "The Nature of Enthusiasm," *Works*, V (New York, 1826), 399.

web of his mind. He must unlearn much of the knowledge which has perhaps constituted hitherto his chief title to superiority.[5]

Opposed to this view of enlightened maturity is, of course, the Romantic attitude or sense of life which reverses the value scale, ignoring historical antecedents and temporality in its attempt to get outside of a fragmented existence in time. This is the synchronic view, admitting co-existence in time, which Emily Brontë has so effectively introduced to Lockwood (and us) in Chapter III. We cannot realize until the end of the novel that our first glimpse of Catherine's hand has been an unconsciously prophetic one:

> This writing, however, was nothing but a name repeated in all kinds of characters, large and small—*Catherine Earnshaw,* here and there varied to *Catherine Heathcliff,* and then again to *Catherine Linton.*

Catherine Earnshaw is to become Catherine Linton in name, Catherine Heathcliff in spirit, then to give birth to another Catherine Linton (a smaller version) who will become another Catherine Earnshaw. Lockwood sees "nothing but a name" (reminding us of Nelly, who at the end has nothing but a name for Heathcliff's grave), but in the childish playing with the name lurk notions of movement and perception that will change the nature of the story.

One consequence of this synchronic view is that the accumulation of knowledge is not necessarily seen as a linear development. What we call experience may be referable in most cases to a linear matrix of chronological order, but the process of living, of moving from "raw" experience to ordered experience is not necessarily cumulative or additive. The past is not strung out "behind" us somewhere, with events strung on it like beads on a string. Part of it stays with us and shapes our experience in the future—which, as Ong points out, is "inside us in a more real sense than it is 'ahead' of us on some metaphoric chronological 'road'." [6]

This is not to prove that Lockwood is wrong, but to emphasize the nature and importance of his actions. The past-as-experience is ultimately childhood, which is "inside" us in the sense described above. But if we cannot leave childhood strung out behind, we can "kill" it, make it history, something that *was,* which is precisely what Lockwood is doing in Chapter IV, and what Catherine and Heathcliff are refusing to have done to them. They will not accept

---

[5] Lord Macauly, quoted in E. L. Tuveson, *Millennium and Utopia* (New York: Harper, 1964), p. 218.

[6] Walker J. Ong, S. J., "The Expanding Humanities and the Individual Scholar," *PMLA, LXXXII* (September, 1967), 4.

being "ranged in a row" for a home-made religious service con-
ducted in "perfect sobriety and silence." They will not accept being
made to "grow up" in a manner that prevents their active involvement with each other and with the world around them. They reject
Lockwood's notion of retirement, Linton's vision of a perfectly calm
heaven, the stability Nelly would like—the whole notion of life
moving towards stasis. So "Th' Helmut uh Salvation" and "T'Brooad
Way to Destruction" are thrown and kicked into the dog-kennel,
along with the frame of mind they represent.

It is after this glimpse of Catherine and Heathcliff's rebellion
that Lockwood begins to dream, and to dream a dream which echoes
it. First, we have the schema of Jabe's sermon, "divided into *four
hundred and ninety* parts, each fully equal to an ordinary address
from the pulpit, and each discussing a separate sin! . . . and it
seemed necessary the brother should sin different sins on every
occasion." This is clearly a *reductio ad absurdum* of the diachronic
existence in time.

> Oh, how weary I grew. How I writhed, and yawned, and nodded,
> and revived! How I pinched and pricked myself, and rubbed my
> eyes, and stood up, and sat down again, and nudged Joseph to inform
> me if he would *ever* have done!
>
> I was condemned to hear all out; finally, he reached the *"First of
> the Seventy-First."* At that crisis, a sudden inspiration descended on
> me; I was moved to rise and denounce Jabes Branderham as the sinner
> of the sin that no Christian need pardon.

Many things are happening here. It is a dream-vision, or poetic
vision of reality, exaggerated and dramatic.[7] Yet it is very much like
a "normal" child's reaction to a long sermon, like Catherine's
reaction to Joseph's sermon on that "awful Sunday." It combines
unusual restraint with unusual violence, and has an ominous
prophetic tone to it, in its suggestion that one leads into the
other, much as Lockwood's exaggerated restraint and decorum have
led to his childish outbreak in the Heights. These are the exaggera-
tions and distortions familiar to everyone in dreams, which com-
monly circumvent the logic and order of conscious experience. But
they are also clearly examples of the dialectical imagination as it
is manifest in art of a certain kind—art that has affinities with the
religious paradox, mysticism, inspiration, and lyric intensity. Even
Lockwood, it would seem, has the possibility within him of re-

[7] The exact state of Lockwood's consciousness in this section is left deliberately
vague, somewhere between sleeping and waking.

awakening his past, of unlocking his visionary powers. Yet he drops
it, and his vision is reduced to the level of naturalistic cause:

> And what was it that had suggested the tremendous tumult, what
> had played Jabe's part in the row? Merely, the branch of a fir-tree that
> touched my lattice, as the blast wailed by, and rattled its dry cones
> against the panes!

Lockwood is terribly close here to the possibility of seizing the wind
as the manifestation of spirit, of a dynamic and substantializing
force, equal to his own spirit of "sudden inspiration," of the "use"
of the wind that we are familiar with in much of Romantic poetry.
In particular, we can compare the poet's position in Shelley's "Ode
to the West Wind" with Lockwood's position by his window:

> The situation of the poet as the poem's protagonist (and the
> protagonist of this poem *must* be a poet) at the close of the first three
> stanzas is that he confronts a choice. He can either surrender himself
> to the wind as an object for it to experience, as the leaf, cloud, and
> wave are objects for it, or else he can attempt to call upon the wind
> to take up a stand in relation to him, to enter into him, and he
> into the wind. This last has nothing to do with any kind of mystical
> union, nor is there any vagueness about it as an aspiration. The poet
> here is confronted by the categories of religious choice: the way of
> despair, which is a submission to the natural process, a dwindling of
> the myth down to object status, a denial of poetry; or another way
> (which on the natural level is also, of course, a way of despair, but
> which at least aspires toward hope), a renewal of myth, an affirmation
> of images and image-making power, a refusal to live with It alone, in
> relation to the wind and whatever is behind the wind.[8]

The wind is a presence throughout *Wuthering Heights*, and we
are made constantly aware of its alternating moods of violence and
calm. But for Lockwood there is never anything "behind" the wind,
as there is nothing "outside" the window. There are only "dry
cones against the panes," like the dead leaves in Shelley's poem.
He chooses the "naturalistic" vision, with its insistence on decline
and decay; his view of religion remains the conscious one of the
decayed chapel without a clergyman, rather than the living experience of his dream with its "full and attentive congregation"
waiting for the outcome of a vital issue. He closes the window on
the little hand, piling the books up as security against its re-entry,
and dismisses the experience as caused by his not having his

---

[8] Harold Bloom, *Shelley's Mythmaking* (New Haven, 1959), p. 84.

She "cannot say why" the memory returns, but she tries manfully, as Lockwood did before the window, to reduce it to its proper perspective. It was childish, involuntary, irresistible; therefore she must have been "cheated . . . into a momentary belief." "Superstition" caused her to read it as "a sign of death," and the whole experience is dismissed as "foolish" when she finds Hareton "not altered greatly since I left him, ten months since." Thus the experience, although it might suggest an almost Wordsworthian moment of vision, succumbs to the "reality" of time. The only justification for including it at all turns out that it happened "about the period" that her narrative had reached at the beginning of the chapter.

Even though Nelly can explain away such experiences, and presume to capture them within the chronological thread of her narrative, there is another side to the time-problem in her narrative. She has not gotten all the "pieces" as they happened; she has them from time-to-time, some of them in an order which has nothing to do with the chronology of the events themselves, but is determined by the chronology of her own experience. Her story is in this sense the history of Nelly Dean discovering the history of Heathcliff, and it is faithful to the development of her piecemeal discoveries rather than to the strict chronological ordering of the events themselves.[10] There is, finally, no history out there (as it appears in Sanger's Appendix) with its own order and logic unless we find it within Nelly's narration.

There is more going on in this confusion than the contrast between "foreground" action scenes and the slow development of a "plot" to contain them, yet this notion has been presented as a way of reading the novel:

In a story where so much takes place at close quarters in immense "foreground" sequences of a few hours or days, and where there are gaps and time shifts, we might tend to ignore the minor incidents and connections. But this is a "history" of two families, whose involved fate is working itself out over three generations. It must be made of resistant material: we must be made aware of the passage of years and of the complex "plot" behind its drama. With these strong links Brontë is free to highlight the most critical events in the lives of Heathcliff and Catherine. By her precise plotting, she succeeds in making us feel the lapse of time without cluttering her story with dates,

[10] This parallels the narratives in Conrad's *Lord Jim* and *Heart of Darkness*, where Marlow is trying to tell *the* story of Jim or Kurtz, but can only tell *his* stories of them.

and holds an involved family history together without losing the
dramatic tension and excitement of an adventure story.[11]

I have quoted Goodridge at length on this point, because he is
so meticulously right in his discoveries of "sequences" and "gaps
and time shifts" (indeed, he follows this paragraph with a page/
date graph of the entire novel!), and so stubbornly wrong about what
to make of the data. We do not know that this is the " 'history' of
two families . . . working itself out over three generations," unless
and until we interpret the book that way, supplying our own notion
of "history" in the process. Brontë does not "make" us feel the lapse
of time in the novel. Readers were (and still are) astonished to
follow Sanger's meticulous chronological reconstruction—so much
so, that they do not realize that it is a *reconstruction,* an invention.

A close look at the sequence from Chapter VII through Chapter
IX should make the point clear. Starting at Christmas (1777), with
Catherine's return from the Grange, we have Heathcliff's decision
to be "good," his failure, his exile and vow to be revenged on
Edgar, the discussion between Nelly and Lockwood, a skip to the
summer of 1778, the birth of Hareton, the death of his mother,
Hindley's commitment to dissipation, a space of two years passed
over without mention, then "one afternoon" in which we see Catherine thinking of marriage with Edgar, the entry of Hindley, his
emotional ambivalence, the dropping of Hareton, Heathcliff's saving
of the child, then his ambivalence, Nelly's catechism of Catherine,
Catherine's dream of heaven (where she would be miserable), her
declaration of love for Heathcliff, his disappearance, her search,
sickness, and delirium, the deaths of both Lintons, the marriage of
Edgar and Catherine (April, 1783), and Nelly's move to the Grange,
leaving Hareton whom she has hardly seen since. This thought
switches the whole novel forward eighteen years in time ("half past
one"), the *past* story is dropped, Heathcliff enters the Grange (while
he is still missing from the history), four weeks of sickness for Lockwood pass, and the history is recommenced by Nelly "on a mellow
evening in September," 1783, when "her hero" returns to the history
and to the Grange.

It is impossible to read this section of the novel with an ordered
feeling of growth-through-time. There is a plausibility to its movement, it flows along, but it does so on an emotional and dialectical
axis rather than a progressive one. That we can look back and date

some of the scenes seems to have little to do with what is really going on. The movement is from Cathy's return from the Grange (transformed, fairy-tale fashion from child to maid, from savage to princess), to Heathcliff's return (also transformed) from wherever he had gone. Lockwood conjectures what Heathcliff may have done during this time, but there is no more knowledge of his "transformation" than there is of his birth and parents. There is nothing in this segment of the novel, or anywhere else, that tells us we *must* see the "history" Goodridge describes as the plot "behind its drama." We could just as well take the constantly present alternative of a fairy-tale plot, and say that it was the basic continuum. In such a plot, chronology and duration are irrelevant, time is merely the medium in which interchangeable patterns repeat themselves, as the second half of the book repeats the first, or the Linton family tree parallels the Earnshaws'.

If we skip from here to the end, we encounter the final and most awkward situation for the chronological historian. For, as we approach the end, we become increasingly aware that the beginning date (fall, 1801) is both a *terminus a quo* and a *terminus ad quem*, that there is the "history" in which Heathcliff is the "hero" and the journal in which Heathcliff must have a different order of existence. It is a shock when Nelly says, "These things happened last winter, sir." (Chapter XXV). We are suddenly reminded that we are trying to get *to* the present to connect these two levels, the past and present, in a narrative continuum. Now we look at Edgar's illness as happening in the spring just before Lockwood arrived at the Grange. Nelly's visit with Cathy to the Heights was in late summer; they were locked up in August, Edgar died in September, Linton Heathcliff died in October, Lockwood began his tenancy and visited the Heights in November, and two days later (November, 1801) Nelly began her story with the summer of 1771. The chronological end of Nelly's story comes in Chapter XXIX, since that concludes all of her first-hand experience of the history. In that chapter Heathcliff visits the Grange, and takes Cathy back to the Heights where Lockwood will find her a month later ("now" a month past). The "actual" time of this chapter is the second week in January, 1802, with Nelly telling about what happened in September, 1801. She is very close to finishing the literal terms of her project, to tell Heathcliff's history up to Lockwood's November visit.

If we look closely at the contents of Chapter XXIX, however, they have very little to do with September, 1801. The chapter is con-

cerned with Heathcliff, whose mind is divided between the future
and the past. He tells Nelly about his discovery of Catherine's ghost,
eighteen years before, and we realize that nothing has changed for
him during those years. "It was a strange way of killing, not by
inches, but by fractions of hair-breadths, to beguile me with the
spectre of a hope, through eighteen years." This hope has been
unchanged since Heathcliff returned from his mysterious absence:

> It was the same room into which he had been ushered, as a guest,
> eighteen years before: the same moon shone through the window;
> and the same autumn landscape lay outside. We had not yet lighted a
> candle, but all the apartment was visible, even to the portraits on the
> wall—the splendid head of Mrs. Linton, and the graceful one of her
> husband.

Nelly emphasizes too that Heathcliff was "the same man," a little
heavier, but "with no other difference." The story has moved along
through the chapters and years, Heathcliff is now owner of the
Grange seeking a tenant, rather than an unwelcome guest, but
nothing of importance has happened to him in all that time;
memory is alive in him, and in us too as we recall that summer
evening. When Heathcliff leaves, he takes Cathy and asks to have
the picture of Catherine sent to the Heights, emphasizing the
parallelism in which Cathy both is, and is not, Catherine. Heathcliff is not trapped in the past, in any simple sense, for he is
also involved now ("yesterday") with preparing Catherine's coffin
for his own interment next to it. He can tell Nelly of both visits
to Catherine's grave, in reverse order, with no significant consequences.

In some way, Nelly's history has failed to give us Heathcliff's
story, although it has been *about* Heathcliff. The next chapter
(XXX) adds nothing except Zillah's account of the six weeks, between Chapter XXIX and the arrival of Lockwood. This brings the
history up to "a little before you came," and is all that Nelly has to
say. We are left, then, with Lockwood's visit (Chapter XXXI) to
announce his departure on "an idle whim" into "the stirring
atmosphere of the town!" This, it must be realized, is the conclusion
of the history of Heathcliff as it was conceived back in Chapter IV.
Lockwood's curiosity has been satisfied, the chronological framework has been laid out connecting the scrawls in the Old Testament
with the people living now in the Heights. This has little to do
with what we have come to think of as Heathcliff's story, yet Lockwood's departure ends the journal report as forcefully as Nelly's

separation from the Heights ended her story. Were it not for the "accident" of Lockwood's return, this would end the novel. With the beginning of Chapter XXXII, we start all over ("1802. —This September I was invited. . . ."). Once again an idle whim or pastime has brought Lockwood to the neighborhood, and on a "sudden impulse" he decides to visit the Heights. With this visit, the whole situation is reversed. "It was sweet warm weather," the air is full of the fragrance of flowers, Cathy and Hareton are in love, there are no barriers or locked doors, and Nelly is in the kitchen singing, while Joseph mumbles complaints:

> "It's a blazing shaime, ut Aw cannut oppen t' Blessed Book, bud yah set up them glories tuh sattan, un' all t' flaysome wickednesses ut iver wer born intuh t' warld! Oh! yah're a raight nowt; un' shoo's another; un' that poor lad 'ull be lost atween ye. Poor lad!" he added, with a groan; "he's witched, Aw'm sartin on 't! O, Lord, judge 'em, fur they's norther law nur justice amang wer rullers!"

He is voicing an ethical-aesthetic criticism of the "story" as well as Nelly's song, because they do not fit his criteria. Nelly answers:

> But wisht, old man, and read your Bible like a christian, and never mind me. This is "Fairy Annie's Wedding"—a bonny tune—it goes to a dance.

The story seems, like the song, to have escaped both the perverse moral structure that Joseph would impose on it, and any connection with the historical structure which Lockwood had woven around it. Lockwood is almost as confused and disoriented this time as he was before, so Nelly brings him ale and "the sequel of Heathcliff's history," in a ministry comparable to her earlier one. She will go into the past, and bring him up to date; she will provide the chronological matrix, at least, for him to connect the seemingly unconnectible. Nelly calls it a "queer" end, and Heathcliff himself refers to it as a "poor conclusion," and "absurd termination to my violent exertions," even though he embraces the "strange change" as an anticipation of his union in death with Catherine.

The novel ends, then, with an air of strangeness, magic and circularity. Nelly's song rings in the air, Hareton and Cathy are united in life as Heathcliff goes to be united with Catherine in death. All the events of the novel are conjured up for us as well as for Nelly (". . . my memory unavoidably recurred to former times with a sort of oppressive sadness.") and once more the past joins the present in a manner that would have satisfied Coleridge:

The common end of all *narrative*, nay, of *all*, Poems is to convert
a *series* into a *Whole*: to make those events, which in real or imagined
History move in a *strait* Line, assume to our Understanding a *circular*
motion—the snake with its Tail in its Mouth.[12]

Lockwood, however, is definitely not satisfied with the conclusion,
and feels "irresistibly impelled to escape . . . again." When he sees
at this point has been commented on endlessly, and must be re-
marked one more time. First, it is a "diversion" which takes him
by the kirk. He is holding in mind the whole story, is under its
sway, yet seems little affected by Nelly's "oppressive sadness" or any
other emotional bent. Lockwood is now going to end the story
he has been writing to himself in his journal. At the kirk, he sees
exactly what he knew he would see when he started there:

> I perceived decay had made progress, even in seven months—many a
> window showed black gaps deprived of glass; and slates jutted off, here
> and there, beyond the right line of the roof, to be gradually worked
> off in coming autumn storms.

He moves on to the three head-stones, for more evidence of the
"progress" of "decay." He lingers pleasantly, wondering "how anyone
could ever imagine unquiet slumbers, for the sleepers in that quiet
earth." This is for him the end of the story; but is it any more
the ending-point, the *terminus ad quem* or resolution of the novel
than Nelly Dean's fairy wedding tune, and the marriage that "will
be on New Year's day"? Lockwood seems content, as many readers
are content with him, at having reached a final stasis in the image
of tranquil death for Catherine and Heathcliff. And, since his is so
clearly an aesthetic satisfaction, a wrapping-up operation, it is easy
to take this as Emily Brontë's ending and her attitude too.

Wylie Sypher has characterized "The limit of the 19th-century
imagination" as "the final expressive tableau, a stasis, a consummate
act," and offered *Wuthering Heights* as evidence for his thesis.[13] In
his view, all 19th-century narratives "culminate with symbolic acts
or gestures," in a "modality of vision" which he calls melodramatic.
The point is useful, because it suggests a way in which each of
the two "stories" we have traced may be seen to end. If our goal
is to understand the novel as Emily Brontë wrote it, however, we
must see that the two modes of vision I have traced exist side-by-side,

---

[12] From a letter to Joseph Cottle, March 7, 1815, in *Collected Letters of
Samuel Taylor Coleridge,* IV (Oxford, 1959), p. 545.
[13] "Aesthetic of Revolution: The Marxist Melodrama," *Kenyon Review*, X
(1948), 433.

not as alternatives from which we must choose, but in relation to an unknown which neither of them fully encompasses. What is outside the window is, literally, the wind, but metaphorically the wind represents the force which makes the world a complex of processes leading to no final solutions or permanent truths. To seek an essence or *anima* in the wind is, finally to intuit that which is "unutterable." But to choose only to see the effects of the wind as they are measurable in time, is to achieve no larger a view of what *is*.

It is only with this recognition that we can truly be ready to read the entire novel and to form a view not of what happens in it, but of how it happens. For what happens is, essentially, a continuous motion from a condition to an opposite condition. Winter is inevitably followed by summer, the births are simultaneous with the deaths, the moments of tranquility follow moments of intense violence—not as separate, isolated states, but as parts of a process. To think of freezing the movement is as strange as the notion of a pendulum swinging only in one direction, or the sound of one hand clapping. The action of the book is a series of shifts, in seasons, lives, and consciousnesses, which imitate and suggest what we can know of the "dynamic and substantializing force" which gives us the wind as an image of itself.[14] For Lockwood to contemplate final tranquility in the graveyard is for him to forget his own observation of the process of change on his return to the Grange ("In winter, nothing more dreary, in summer, nothing more divine. . . .") and to ignore the implications of his other observation on the way to the Heights:

> . . . so I turned away and made my exit, rambling leisurely along, with the glow of a sinking sun behind, and the mild glory of a rising moon in front; one fading, and the other brightening, as I quitted the park, and climbed the stony by-road branching off to Mr. Heathcliff's dwelling.

The whole novel is full of such images of change on a small scale, which suggest a larger process of change in the very nature of things. Not a sharp, radical change, but a constant process or

[14] I have borrowed the phrase from one of Yeats' letters to Florence Farr: "I have myself by the by begun eastern meditations—of your sort, but with the object of trying to lay hands upon some dynamic and substantializing force as distinguished from the eastern quiescent and supersensualizing state of the soul—a movement downwards upon life, not upwards out of life." *The Letters of W. B. Yeats* (New York: Macmillan, 1954), p. 469.

movement between extremes which are isolated moments in the
process, mental abstractions which we bring to it. As Lockwood
moves still closer to the mystery of the Heights, he overhears Cathy
giving Hareton a lesson:

> "Con-*trary!*" said a voice, as sweet as a silver bell—"That for the third
> time, you dunce! I'm not going to tell you, again—Recollect, or I
> pull your hair!"
> "Contrary, then," answered another, in deep, but softened tones. "And
> now, kiss me, for minding so well."
> "No, read it first correctly, without a single mistake."

Hareton reads, but as his attention strays, it is recalled by "a
smart slap on the cheek." Lockwood looks in on this scene as Satan
watched Adam and Eve in the Garden, recognizing it as bliss, know-
ing he is excluded, but unable to see the lesson before him. "I bit
my lip, in spite, at having thrown away the chance I might have
had, of doing something besides staring at its smiting beauty."

It is no accident, then, that the subject of the lesson is to master
the word "contrary," or that the scene comes at the end of the book.
It is not a lesson that is led up to and revealed, however, but one
that has been before our eyes from the very beginning, in every
scene and every event.[15] It is the "lesson" made visible over the door
to the Heights:

> Before passing the threshold, I paused to admire a quantity of
> grotesque carving lavished over the front, and especially about the
> principal door, above which, among a wilderness of crumbling griffins
> and shameless little boys, I detected the date "1500," and the name
> "Hareton Earnshaw." I would have made a few comments, and re-
> quested a short history of the place from the surly owner, but his
> attitude at the door appeared to demand my speedy entrance, or com-
> plete departure, and I had no desire to aggravate his impatience
> previous to inspecting the penetralium.

Lockwood's "inspection" is fruitless for him, even after a long
history, for his mind is already shaped. The date and crumbling
griffins suggest the one principle of change he knows and will
recognize. But the little boys, shamelessly asserting their youth and
renewed energy must be dismissed or explained away.

[15] Chapter XXIV offers an especially striking anticipation. There we have the
"contrary" states of Linton's heaven ("an ecstacy of peace") and Catherine's
("the whole world awake and wild with joy"), followed by Hareton's attempt
to read the legend above the door to the Heights. He can read the name
(his own) but not the date!

There is one final danger, even after recognizing the importance of contraries and the process of change as the reality behind the events which "happen" in the novel. We are still tempted to look for a resolution in artistic terms, to read the novel as the writer's attempt to resolve the contraries of life. This tendency can partly be overcome by divorcing ourselves from Lockwood, who tends to trap us both as narrator and as an image of ourselves. It can also be overcome by recognizing the important literary affinities of the novel, and of Emily Brontë's imagination. Her desire and her vision are close to Blake, perhaps most obviously in his "Marriage of Heaven and Hell," where the "marriage" is not a state but a constant process in which "one portion of being is the Prolific, the other the Devouring." She shares this intuitive vision with the other Romantics, obviously, but also with the other thinkers and writers since Blake who have struggled with models or theories of process, change, and evolution, in hopes of finding in the Heraclitean fire of nature something of what Hopkins meant by the "Comfort of the Resurrection."

> But the mingled, mingling threads of life are woven by warp and woof: calms crossed by storms, a storm for every calm. There is no steady unretracing progress in this life; we do not advance through infancy's unconscious spell, boyhood's thoughtless faith, adolescence' doubt (the common doom), then scepticism, then disbelief, resting at last in manhood's pondering repose of If. But once gone through, we trace the round again; and are infants, boys, and men, and Ifs eternally.[16]

[16] *Moby Dick,* Chapter CXIV (New York: Bobbs-Merrill, 1964), p. 624.

PART TWO

View Points

Virginia Woolf: Jane Eyre and *Wuthering Heights*

Wuthering Heights is a more difficult book to understand than *Jane Eyre*, because Emily was a greater poet than Charlotte. When Charlotte wrote she said with eloquence and splendor and passion "I love," "I hate," "I suffer." Her experience, though more intense, is on a level with our own. But there is no "I" in *Wuthering Heights*. There are no governesses. There are no employers. There is love, but it is not the love of men and women. Emily was inspired by some more general conception. The impulse which urged her to create was not her own suffering or her own injuries. She looked out upon a world cleft into gigantic disorder and felt within her the power to unite it in a book. That gigantic ambition is to be felt throughout the novel—a struggle, half thwarted but of superb conviction, to say something through the mouths of her characters which is not merely "I love" or "I hate," but "we, the whole human race" and "you, the eternal powers . . ." the sentence remains unfinished. It is not strange that it should be so; rather it is astonishing that she can make us feel what she had it in her to say at all. It surges up in the half-articulate words of Catherine Earnshaw, "If all else perished and *he* remained, I should still continue to be; and if all else remained and he were annihilated, the universe would turn to a mighty stranger; I should not seem part of it." It breaks out again in the presence of the dead. "I see a repose that neither earth nor hell can break, and I feel an assurance of the endless and shadowless hereafter—the eternity they have entered—where life is boundless in its duration, and love in its sympathy and joy in its fulness." It is this suggestion of power underlying the apparitions of human nature, and lifting them up into the presence of greatness that gives the book its huge stature

among other novels. But it was not enough for Emily Brontë to
write a few lyrics, to utter a cry, to express a creed. In her poems
she did this once and for all, and her poems will perhaps outlast
her novel. But she was novelist as well as poet. She must take upon
herself a more laborious and a more ungrateful task. She must
face the fact of other existences, grapple with the mechanism of
external things, build up, in recognizable shape, farms and houses
and report the speeches of men and women who existed independ-
ently of herself. And so we reach these summits of emotion not by
rant or rhapsody but by hearing a girl sing old songs to herself
as she rocks in the branches of a tree; by watching the moor sheep
crop the turf; by listening to the soft wind breathing through the
grass. The life at the farm with all its absurdities and its im-
probability is laid open to us. We are given every opportunity of
comparing *Wuthering Heights* with a real farm and Heathcliff with
a real man. How, we are allowed to ask, can there be truth or
insight or the finer shades of emotion in men and women who so
little resemble what we have seen ourselves? But even as we ask it
we see in Heathcliff the brother that a sister of genius might have
seen; he is impossible we say, but nevertheless no boy in literature
has so vivid an existence as his. So it is with the two Catherines;
never could women feel as they do or act in their manner, we say.
All the same, they are the most lovable women in English fiction.
It is as if she could tear up all that we know human beings by, and
fill these unrecognizable transparences with such a gust of life that
they transcend reality. Hers, then, is the rarest of all powers. She
could free life from its dependence on facts; with a few touches
indicate the spirit of a face so that it needs no body; by speaking of
the moor make the wind blow and the thunder roar.

David Cecil: Emily Brontë and *Wuthering Heights*

The setting is a microcosm of the universal scheme as Emily Brontë
conceived it. On the one hand, we have Wuthering Heights, the
land of storm; high on the barren moorland, naked to the shock
of the elements, the natural home of the Earnshaw family, fiery,

"Emily Brontë and Wuthering Heights," from Early Victorian Novelists *by
David Cecil. Copyright 1935 by the Bobbs-Merrill Company, Inc. Reprinted by
permission of the Bobbs-Merrill Company, Inc.*

untamed children of the storm. On the other, sheltered in the leafy valley below, stands Thrushcross Grange, the appropriate home of the children of calm, the gentle, passive, timid Lintons. Together each group, following its own nature in its own sphere, combines to compose a cosmic harmony. It is the destruction and re-establishment of this harmony which is the theme of the story. It opens with the arrival at Wuthering Heights of an extraneous element— Heathcliff. He, too, is a child of the storm; and the affinity between him and Catherine Earnshaw makes them fall in love with each other. But since he is an extraneous element, he is a source of discord, inevitably disrupting the working of the natural order. He drives the father, Earnshaw, into conflict with the son, Hindley, and as a result Hindley into conflict with himself, Heathcliff. The order is still further dislocated by Catherine, who is seduced into uniting herself in an "unnatural" marriage with Linton, the child of calm. The shock of her infidelity and Hindley's ill-treatment of him now, in its turn, disturbs the natural harmony of Heathcliff's nature, and turns him from an alien element in the established order, into a force active for its destruction. He is not therefore, as usually supposed, a wicked man voluntarily yielding to his wicked impulses. Like all Emily Brontë's characters, he is a manifestation of natural forces acting involuntarily under the pressure of his own nature. But he is a natural force which has been frustrated of its natural outlet, so that it inevitably becomes destructive; like a mountain torrent diverted from its channel, which flows out on the surrounding country, laying waste whatever may happen to lie in its way. Nor can it stop doing so, until the obstacles which kept it from its natural channel are removed.

Heathcliff's first destructive act is to drive Hindley to death. Secondly, as a counterblast to Catherine's marriage, and actuated not by love, but by hatred of the Lintons, he himself makes another "unnatural" marriage with Isabella. This, coupled with the conflict induced in her by her own violation of her nature, is too much for Catherine; and she dies. Heathcliff, further maddened by the loss of his life's object, becomes yet more destructive, and proceeds to wreak his revenge on the next generation, Hareton Earnshaw, Catherine Linton and Linton Heathcliff. These—for Hindley, like Heathcliff and Catherine, had married a child of calm—cannot be divided as their parents were into children of calm or storm; they are the offspring of both and partake of both natures. But there is a difference between them. Hareton and Catherine are the children of love, and so combine the positive "good" qualities of

their respective parents: the kindness and constancy of calm, the
strength and courage of storm. Linton, on the other hand, is a
child of hate, and combines the negative "bad" qualities of his two
parents—the cowardice and weakness of calm, the cruelty and ruthlessness of storm.[1] Heathcliff obtains power over all three children.
Catherine is married to her natural antipathy, Linton; so that her
own nature, diverted from its purpose, grows antagonistic to her
natural affinity—Hareton. The natural order is for the time being
wholly subverted: the destructive principle reigns supreme. But at
this, its high-water mark, the tide turns. From this moment the
single purpose that directs the universe begins to reassert itself, to
impose order once more. First of all Linton Heathcliff dies. Negative as his nature is, it has not the seed of life within it. Then, freed
from the incubus of his presence, the affinity between Hareton
and Catherine begins to override the superficial antagonism that
Heathcliff's actions have raised between them; they fall in love. The
only obstacle left to the re-establishment of harmony is Heathcliff's
antagonism; finally this, too, changes. His nature could never find
fulfillment in destruction; for it was not—as we have seen—primarily
destructive, and has become so only because it was frustrated
of its true fulfillment—union with its affinity, Catherine Earnshaw.
Heathcliff's desire for this union never ceased to torment him.
Even at his most destructive, her magnetic power dragged at his
heart, depriving him of any sense of satisfaction his revenge might
have obtained for him. Now it grows so strong that it breaks
through the veil of mortality to manifest itself to his physical eye
in the shape of her ghost. The actual sight of her gives him strength
at last to defeat the forces that had upset his equilibrium; with a
prodigious effort the stream breaks through the obstacles that had
so long stood in its way, and flows at last in a torrent down its rightful channel. He forgets his rage, he forgets even to satisfy the wants
of physical nature; he wants only to unite himself with Catherine.
Within two days his wish is satisfied. He dies. His death removes the
last impediment to the re-establishment of harmony. Hareton and
Catherine settle down happy and united at Thrushcross Grange.
Wuthering Heights is left to its rightful possessors, the spirits of

---

[1] Of course, this is true only in a broad sense. Emily Brontë has too great a sense
of reality to create unmitigated villains or impeccable heroes. Moreover, all
three children springing as they do from "unnatural" unions are not perfectly
homogeneous characters. Hareton can be surly, Catherine wilful. And Linton—
for his mother loved his father first, if only with a physical passion—is touched
at times with a redeeming gleam of pathos.

Heathcliff and the first Catherine. The wheel has come full circle; at length the alien element that has so long disturbed it has been assimilated to the body of nature; the cosmic order has been established once more.

Dorothy Van Ghent: On *Wuthering Heights*

Essentially, *Wuthering Heights* exists for the mind as a tension between two kinds of reality: the raw, inhuman reality of anonymous natural energies, and the restrictive reality of civilized habits, manners, and codes. The first kind of reality is given to the imagination in the violent figures of Catherine and Heathcliff, portions of the flux of nature, children of rock and heath and tempest, striving to identify themselves as human, but disrupting all around them with their monstrous appetite for an inhuman kind of intercourse, and finally disintegrated from within by the very energies out of which they are made. It is this vision of a reality radically alien from the human that the ancient Chinese landscape paintings offer also. But in those ancient paintings there is often a tiny human figure, a figure that is obviously that of a philosopher, for instance, or that of a peasant—in other words, a human figure decisively belonging to and representing a culture—who is placed in diminutive perspective beside the enormously cascading torrent, or who is seen driving his water buffalo through the overwhelming mists or faceless snows; and this figure is outlined sharply, so that, though it is extremely tiny, it is very definite in the giant surrounding indefiniteness. The effect is one of contrast between finite and infinite, between the limitation of the known and human, and the unlimitedness of the unknown and nonhuman. So also in *Wuthering Heights:* set over against the wilderness of inhuman reality is the quietly secular, voluntarily limited, safely human reality that we find in the gossipy concourse of Nelly Dean and Lockwood, the one an old family servant with a strong grip on the necessary emotional economies that make life endurable, the other a city visitor in the country, a man whose very disinterestedness and facility of feeling

and attention indicate the manifold emotional economies by which
city people particularly protect themselves from any disturbing note
of the ironic discord between civilized life and the insentient wild
flux of nature in which it is islanded. This second kind of reality
is given also in the romance of Cathy and Hareton, where book
learning and gentled manners and domestic charities form a little
island of complacence. The tension between these two kinds of
reality, their inveterate opposition and at the same time their
continuity one with another, provides at once the content and the
form of *Wuthering Heights.*

Edgar F. Shannon, Jr.: Lockwood's Dreams and
the Exegesis of *Wuthering Heights*

In two successive visits to Wuthering Heights, Lockwood, gregari-
ous and affable, is the object of rebuffs and indignities. Detained by
the snowfall, he is refused both a guide to the Grange and a bed in
the house. During each of his calls ferocious dogs attack him; and
on the second occasion, while Gnasher and Wolf pin him to the
ground, Heathcliff and Hareton laugh at his predicament. His
nose bleeds, and Zillah finally checks the gore by dashing a pint of
freezing water down his neck. He goes to bed cold, dizzy, nauseated,
and, not surprisingly, in a "bad temper". His two dreams, though
immediately induced by his reading and the rapping branch, emo-
tionally derive from the events of the past two days; and the assault
of Branderham's congregation provides a penultimate instance of
violence to Lockwood's person.

In this dream, having "no weapon to raise in self-defense," he
begins grappling with Joseph for his staff. Despite the conspiracy
of critics to present him as a milksop, Lockwood habitually reacts
swiftly and responds aggressively to abuse. When the bitch flies
at him on his first visit, he flings her back, interposes a table
between himself and the swarm of curs, and holds off his principal
assailants with a poker. Thinking that a derogatory remark of
Joseph's to young Catherine is meant for him, he is "sufficiently

"*Lockwood's Dreams and the Exegesis of* Wuthering Heights," *from* Nine-
teenth-Century Fiction, *XIV, 2 (September, 1959).* © *1959 by The Regents of
The University of California. Reprinted by permission of The Regents and
Edgar F. Shannon, Jr.*

enraged" to step "towards the aged rascal with an intention of kicking him out of the door." Discovering that Heathcliff will not allow Hareton to be his guide in the snow, he snatches the lantern by which Joseph is milking and starts off alone. When the dogs pull him down and stand over him, he trembles, not in fear but in rage, and shouts imprecations at them and at Heathcliff until Zillah intervenes.

Lockwood's frantic attempt in the nightmare to break Cathy's grip by cutting her wrist on the broken glass "till the blood ran down and soaked the bedclothes" is not, then, as Mrs. Van Ghent maintains, mere gratuitous cruelty, psychologically unmotivated.[1] He had already shown himself capable of giving pain and had "gained a reputation of deliberate heartlessness" when he disdained and discomfited the young lady at the sea coast who had finally returned his visual advances. But his barbarity to the child grows out of the first dream and is an ultimate act of self-assertion and self-preservation—the final terrified retaliation of the dreamer for the physical and emotional outrages he has sustained.

Clearly, there is little foundation for Mrs. Van Ghent's contention that the very lack of motivation for Lockwood's action substantiates the symbolic quality of the nightmare as a revelation of autonomous darkness in the psychic depths of the human soul, even in the soul of a character who "more successfully than anyone else in the book, has shut out the powers of darkness." [2] Rather, the dream is symptomatic of the careful causality that governs the central action of the novel. When Lockwood contends that people in remote regions "*do* live more in earnest, more in themselves, and less in surface, change, and frivolous external things" than city dwellers, Nelly replies, "Oh! here we are the same as anywhere else, when you get to know us." This exchange embodies the novelist's claim for the scope of the representation. Lockwood demonstrates in little what occurs in gigantic proportions in Heathcliff. The cruelty in the nightmare indicates that all men—sophisticate as well as boor—react vehemently to exacerbation of nerves and negation of sympathy. Repelled, even Lockwood's well-bred gestures toward social intercourse overnight degenerate into brutality.

[1] "On *Wuthering Heights*," in *The English Novel: Form and Function* (New York, 1953), p. 160.
[2] *Ibid.*, p. 161.

V. S. Pritchett: Implacable, Belligerent People of Emily Brontë's Novel, *Wuthering Heights*

I have been reading *Wuthering Heights* again, after 20 years, a novel which is often regarded as poetical, mystical and fabulous. No people like Heathcliff and Catherine, it is said, ever existed. *Wuthering Heights* is indeed a poetical novel; but when I was reading it, it seemed to me the most realistic statement about the Yorkshire people of the isolated moorland and dales that I have ever read. I am a southerner; but I spent a good deal of my childhood in those Northern cottages and I recognize the implacable, belligerent people of Emily Brontë's novel at once. The trap used to pick you up at the branch line station and in a few miles you were on the moors, the wind standing against you like an enemy, the moorland drizzle making wraiths over the endless scene, and the birds whimpering in cries of farewell, like parting ghosts. Austere, empty, ominous were the earth and sky, and the air was fiercer and more violent than in the South. The occasional small stone houses stuck up like forts, the people themselves seemed, to a southerner, as stern as soldiers, and even the common sentences they spoke were so turned that, but for a quizzical glitter in the eyes of the speaker, one might have taken their words as challenge, insult or derision. I do not mean that these remote Yorkshire people were not kindly and hospitable folk; but one had not to live among them for long, before one found that their egotism was naked, their hatred unending. They seemed to revel in an hostility which they called frankness or bluntness; but which—how can I put it?—was an attempt to plant all they were, all they could be, all they represented as people, unyieldingly before you. They expected you to do the same. They despised you if you did not. They had the combative pride of clansmen and, on their lonely farms, clans they were and had been for hundreds of years. I can think of episodes in my own childhood among them which are as extraordinary as some of the things in *Wuthering Heights;* and which, at first sight, would strike the reader as examples of pitiable hatred and harshness. Often

"*Implacable, Belligerent People of Emily Brontë's Novel,* Wuthering Heights," *from* New Statesman and Nation, *XXI (June 22, 1946). Reprinted by permission of Statesman and Nation Publishing Co.*

they were. But really their fierceness in criticism, the pride, and the violence of their sense of sin was the expression of a view of life which put energy and the will of man above everything else. To survive in these parts, one had to dominate and oppose.

There is no other novel in the English language like *Wuthering Heights*. It is unique first of all for its lack of psychological dismay. Never, in a novel, did so many people hate each other with such zest, such Northern zest. There is a faint, homely pretense that Nelly, the housekeeper and narrator, is a kindly, garrulous old body; but look at her. It is not concealed that she is a spy, a go-between, a secret opener of letters. She is a wonderful character, as clear and round as any old nurse in Richardson or Scott; but no conventional sentiment encases her. She is as hard as iron and takes up her station automatically in the battle. Everyone hates, no one disguises evil in this book; no one is "nice." How refreshing it is to come across a Victorian novel which does not moralize, and yet is very far from amoral. How strange, in Victorian fiction, to see passion treated as the natural pattern of life. How refreshing to see the open skirmishing of egotism, and to see life crackling like a fire through human beings; a book which *feels* human beings as they feel to themselves.

David Daiches: Introduction to *Wuthering Heights*

Most readers will agree that the intrusion of Heathcliff into the affairs of Wuthering Heights and Thrushcross Grange and his vital *rapport* with the elder Catherine represent a deeply imagined and vividly presented awareness of some profound and ambiguous force working in man and nature. They will agree, too, that the moorland setting and the effortlessly brilliant way in which human passions are related to aspects of natural activity in this moorland landscape give the novel a power beyond anything which the action itself can convey. The most powerful, the most irresistible, and the most tenacious of forces that reside in the depths of human nature have no relation with the artificial world of civilization and gentility, but they do have a relation to the elemental forces at work in the natural world and also to the impulse to provide the

Introduction to Wuthering Heights *(Baltimore, Penguin Books, 1965). Copyright 1965 by David Daiches. Reprinted by permission of Penguin Books, Ltd.*

basic elements of a civilized life—fire and food. There is also the recurrent and disturbing suggestion that the depths of man's nature are in some way alien to him. Heathcliff comes from a mysterious outside and finds his natural mate in the inhabitant of an ordinary moorland farmhouse. We might almost say that one of the insights achieved by the novel is that what is most natural is by very virtue of its being most natural also most unnatural. Man is both at home and not at home in nature. He is capable of perversions and cruelties that are not found in nature, but that is because he is urged on by deep natural forces within him which find themselves at odds with the demands of convention and even of ordinary humanness.

It is perhaps curious that Emily Brontë shows no sense of the otherness of the other person in a passionate relationship between the sexes. Ultimate passion is for her rather a kind of recognition of one's self—one's true and absolute self—in the object of passion. ("Nelly, I *am* Heathcliff." "I *cannot* live without my life! I *cannot* live without my soul!") This notion makes contact with the suggestions of incest in the novel (Heathcliff and Catherine had been brought up as brother and sister) to suggest a kind of *hoarding* of passion which is related perhaps to Heathcliff's later avarice and to the Thomistic explanation of incest as a form of avarice (for it selfishly keeps love within the family and does not offer it to someone outside).

Eric Solomon: The Incest Theme in
Wuthering Heights

In Nelly Dean's narrative, no reason is suggested for Earnshaw's visit to Liverpool, and this in a passage where Nelly describes not only the distance, "sixty miles each way," [1] and the fact that he is going to make the journey on foot, but also the gifts—a fiddle and a whip—to be purchased for Hindley and Cathy. These details are presented clearly, but Nelly never so much as indicates why Earn-

"The Incest Theme in Wuthering Heights," *from* Nineteenth-Century Fiction, *XIV, 1 (June, 1959).* © *1959 by The Regents of the University of California. Reprinted by permission of The Regents and Eric Solomon.*

[1] All citations to *Wuthering Heights* refer to Chapter IV of Emily Brontë, *Wuthering Heights* (Oxford, 1931) [The Shakespeare Head Brontë]. Italics in passages quoted are mine.

shaw is making this arduous trip, whether in connection with the farm, legal matters, or personal reasons.

Earnshaw returns with a mysterious dirty child whom his wife "must e'en take as a gift of God." He gives a vague and illogical report of finding the homeless and starving child in the Liverpool gutters. Earnshaw's rationalization of the adoption seems weak:

> Not a soul knew to whom it belonged, he said, and his money and time, being both limited, he thought it better to take it home with him, at once, than run into vain expenses there; because he was determined he would not leave it as he found it.

Even in an eighteenth-century provincial slum, the waif must have had *some* protector. Mrs. Earnshaw considers her husband to be mad, and the narrator, tart Nelly Dean, expresses doubts through her manner of recounting the tale. She informs Lockwood that Earnshaw "*tried* to explain the matter; but he was *really* half dead with fatigue . . . all that I could make out . . . was a *tale* of his seeing it . . ."

The brief picture of Mrs. Earnshaw presented here would certainly supply an added motive for concealment of a child who could possibly be Earnshaw's illegitimate offspring. She "was ready to fling it out of doors"; she grumbles and berates the exhausted traveler. How would such a woman have reacted to any honest admission of sinful adultery? [2] Earnshaw could only bring a by-blow into the family by devious means, as long as his wife was still alive.

In addition, Heathcliff soon becomes Earnshaw's favorite, more cherished than his own children, an unnatural occurrence surely— unless this is a natural child. Nelly has her suspicions. Earnshaw, she comments, "took to the child *strangely,*" this "poor fatherless child, as *he* called him." Hindley, for his part, sees Heathcliff "as a usurper of his parent's affections."

There can be no doubt that Emily Brontë cast a vague incestuous aura over the entire plot of *Wuthering Heights*. Heathcliff marries his lost love's sister-in-law; his wife's son marries her brother's daughter; Cathy's daughter marries *her* brother's son. An uncon-

---

[2] It might be objected at this point that Earnshaw hardly seems the type of man who would have a clandestine affair to conceal. One can, however, derive Emily Brontë's belief in heredity from the strong family resemblances displayed by her characters. The second generation of Heathcliffs and Lintons markedly show the parents' characteristics. Since Cathy and Hindley, Earnshaw's legitimate children, display the wild and drunken natures that their author assigns them, might not this indicate something about her view of the parent, something not incommensurate with siring an illegitimate child?

sciously incestuous love between the two leading characters would
not run counter to the tone of a novel filled with violent and savage
scenes, such as the sadistic rubbing of a wrist over a broken window-
pane, Cathy's fierce delirium, or the sight of Heathcliff smashing his
bloody head against a tree.

Irving H. Buchen: Emily Brontë and the Metaphysics of Childhood and Love

What should be noted at the outset, however, is that the love experience, far from being unrelated to childhood, resembles and even
grows out of it. The poem which perhaps best illustrates this relationship is "The Death of A.G.A.," especially these lines:

> "Listen; I've known a burning heart
> To which my own was given;
> Nay, not in passion; do not start—
> Our love was love from heaven;
> At least, if heavenly love be born
> In the pure light of childhood's morn—
> Long ere the prison-tainted air
> From this world's plague-fen rises there.
>
> My soul dwelt with her day and night:
> She was my all-sufficing light,
> My childhood's mate, my girlhood's guide,
> My only blessing, only pride." [1]

To be sure, there is something radical and perhaps even out-
rageous in endowing children with the capacity to sustain a relationship normally reserved for adults. And yet does not this linkage in
the poems serve to remind us that *Wuthering Heights* is essentially
a novel about children? The bulk of the story concerns itself with
the infancy and early years first of Heathcliff, Catherine, Edgar, and
Isabella; and later of Linton, Cathy, and Hareton. And even when
each generation grows up they are not so much adults as arrested

"*Emily Brontë and the Metaphysics of Childhood and Love,*" *from* Nineteenth-
Century Fiction, *XXII, 1 (June, 1967).* © *1967 by the Regents of The University
of California. Reprinted by permission of The Regents and Irving H. Buchen.*

[1] *The Complete Poems of Emily Jane Brontë,* edited by C. W. Hatfield (London,
1941), pp. 152-53.

children. Indeed, when Heathcliff and Catherine are reunited, Catherine appears to regress toward childhood. Her tantrums lead Nelly to say that Catherine seemed "to find childish diversion in pulling the feathers from the rents she had just made" in the pillow. Nelly pleads with Catherine to " 'Give over with that baby-work' " and soon after describes her behavior by saying "our fiery Catherine was no better than a wailing child." Even the civilized Isabella evidences similar fits. Visiting Nelly, she throws off her wedding ring and cries out, " 'I'll smash it!' she continued, striking with childish spite." And much later when love flowers between Hareton and Cathy, Nelly's reminder that she is eighteen and he twenty-three comes as a surprise; for their actions seem more like those of children than adults. The only real adults in the novel are the original Mr. and Mrs. Earnshaw and Mr. and Mrs. Linton. But they are shadowy figures and depart soon after the novel begins. Joseph and Nelly exist on the periphery of the story; moreover, they give the impression of being ancients or always old.

Thus, although the novel conveys the sense of progress because of its complex forward movement and its span of three generations, it never really moves away from its preoccupation with childhood. This recurrent focus, in fact, is primarily responsible for the novel's special achievement of timelessness. Or to put it another way, because the novel is polarized between a constant revelation of the past and a constant anticipation of the future, there is no real sense of the present. The focus on paradise lost and paradise regained is so total and tyrannical that, just as there are no genuine moments of temporality, so there are no conditions of secularity. As an unexpected but logical correlation, there is no sex. To be sure, there is love—an uncompromising, agonized yearning of one soul for another—but it is never corporeal just as it is never temporal.

It is at this point that the connections between childhood and love may be suggested. Consistently, Brontë speaks of the disuniting of lovers or the loss of love in the same terms and with the same dimensions that she speaks of the separation of the child from God or his loss of heaven. Thus, the separation of Heathcliff and Catherine from each other reenacts the initial exile from God and the initial state of being born. That such divorce in fact occurs in their childhood is not just a coincidental but a symbolic reinforcement. Nowhere is this more dramatically presented than when the married Catherine tries to indicate to Nelly the extent of the gulf she now feels in her life:

"But, supposing at twelve years old, I had been wrenched from the Heights, and every early association, and my all in all, as Heathcliff was at that time, and been converted at a stroke into Mrs. Linton, the lady of Thrushcross Grange, and the wife of a stranger; an exile, and outcast, thence-forth, from what had been my world . . ."

Catherine's description of the loss both of Wuthering Heights and of Heathcliff's love could be applied without any revision to the child's loss of heaven and the event of birth. The notion of traumatic discontinuity with all that was as well as all the terms the lovers use to describe it—hell, exile, imprisonment, death—are precisely the familiar terms employed in the poems to describe the child's entry into this dungeon world.

J. Hillis Miller: Emily Brontë

Cathy and Heathcliff reach in death what they possessed in this world when they were unself-conscious children, and did not know of their separateness. They reach peace not through obedient acceptance of isolation, but through the final exhaustion of all their forces in the attempt to reach union in this life. Their heroism is, in George Bataille's phrase, an "approbation of life to the point of death." [1] Cathy's death is caused by their embrace: "An instant they held asunder; and then how they met I hardly saw, but Catherine made a spring, and he caught her, and they were locked in an embrace from which I thought my mistress would never be released alive. In fact, to my eyes, she seemed directly insensible." Heathcliff too reaches death through the exhaustion of his vitality. This exhaustion is brought about by his frantic attempt to reach Cathy's ghost: "I have to remind myself to breathe—almost to remind my heart to beat! And it is like bending back a stiff spring . . . it is by compulsion, that I do the slightest act, not prompted by one thought, and by compulsion, that I notice anything alive, or dead, which is not associated with one universal idea . . . I have a single wish, and my whole being, and faculties are yearning to attain it.

"*Emily Brontë,*" *from* The Disappearance of God: Five Nineteenth-Century Writers. *Copyright 1963 by the President and Fellows of Harvard College. Reprinted by permission of The Belknap Press of Harvard University Press.*

[1] "L'érotisme est," writes Bataille in his excellent essay on Emily Brontë, ". . . l'approbation de la vie jusque dans la mort" (*La littérature et le mal* [Paris, 1957], p. 12).

They have yearned towards it so long, and so unwaveringly, that I'm convinced it *will* be reached—and *soon*—because it has devoured my existence—I am swallowed in the anticipation of its fulfilment"; ". . . you might as well bid a man struggling in the water, rest within arms-length of the shore! I must reach it first, and then I'll rest."

At the end of *Wuthering Heights* Cathy and Heathcliff have reached the peace of union with one another through God, a God who is at once immanent and transcendent, utterly beyond this world, "brooding above" it, and within it as what "pervades" it everywhere, just as the soft breeze breathes over the moors in the last paragraph of the novel. One need not, as Lockwood says, "imagine unquiet slumbers, for the sleepers in that quiet earth," and "under that benign sky." Only in death, the realm of absolute communion, can Heathcliff "dissolve with" Cathy and "be happy" at last. The final happiness of Cathy and Heathcliff, like their first union in childhood, can only be spoken of symbolically. The tremendous storm raised by the separation of the two lovers, a storm which has swirled out to engulf all the characters in the novel, has been appeased at last, and calm has returned. Heathcliff has broken through to the still point at the center of the whirlwind, the divine point where all opposites are reconciled and where he can possess Cathy again because he possesses all things in God. The calm he has reached has spread back into the world to be tangible in the soft wind breathing through the grass and blowing through the open windows at Wuthering Heights. Emanations from the center of peace have been liberated to flow out to the periphery of the circle, and to irradiate all the world with a benign and pervasive glow. The state of savagery in which Lockwood first found the people at Wuthering Heights has been transcended at last.

Chronology of Important Dates

The Brontës	The Age
1818 Emily Jane Brontë born, July 30.	Birth of Karl Marx; first steamship crossing of Atlantic.
1820 The Brontës move to Haworth.	George III dies; Malthus publishes *Principles of Political Economy*.
1824 Maria and Elizabeth Brontë go to school at Cowan Bridge in July, Charlotte in August, Emily in November.	Repeal of Combination Acts in Great Britain.
1825 Maria and Elizabeth die; Charlotte and Emily withdrawn from school.	Decembrist revolt in Russia; twelve-hour workday established in England for children under 16.
1826 Mr. Brontë brings home the famous wooden soldiers from Branwell.	Final independence of the Spanish-American colonies.
1831 Charlotte goes to school at Roe Head. Emily and Anne begin Gondal.	
1835 Charlotte returns to Roe Head as governess; Emily goes as pupil, leaves ill and homesick after 3 months.	
1836	Publication of R. W. Emerson's *Nature*, beginning of Transcendentalists in America.
1837 Emily becomes governess at Miss Patchett's school (Law Hill, near Halifax). Stays for several months.	Victoria begins her reign.
1841 The three sisters, living together at Haworth, plan to start their own school.	

The Brontës	*The Age*
1842 Charlotte and Emily go to Brussels to study. Emily stays 8 months.	Phineas T. Barnum opens Barnum's American Museum in New York.
1844 Circulars advertising the Brontë sisters' proposed school elicit no response.	Rochdale pioneers found Co-operative Society.
1845 Charlotte discovers Emily's poems. Plans formed for publishing poems and novels.	Engels publishes *The Condition of the Working Classes in England.*
1846 *Poems,* by Currer, Ellis and Acton Bell published; *Wuthering Heights* and *Agnes Grey* in December.	Repeal of Corn Laws in England; U.S. War with Mexico.
1848 Emily Brontë dies, December 19.	Marx and Engels issue *The Communist Manifesto.* Revolutions in France, Germany, Austria, Italy, Hungary.
1850 The second edition of *Wuthering Heights,* edited by Charlotte Brontë, with "Biographical Notice of Ellis and Acton Bell."	Tennyson succeeds Wordsworth as poet laureate.
1851	The Great Exhibition in Hyde Park, London (Joseph Paxton's Crystal Palace).

Notes on the Editor and Authors

Thomas A. Vogler, the editor, is Associate Professor of Literature at the University of California at Santa Cruz.

Irving H. Buchen is an Assistant Professor of English, Fairleigh Dickinson University, Madison, New Jersey.

Lord David Cecil is Goldsmith Professor of English Literature at the University of Oxford. He is a distinguished literary critic and historian, and the author of many books. Among his recent publications are *Modern Verse in England, 1900–1950*, and *The Fine Art of Reading*.

David Daiches is Professor of English at the University of Sussex. A distinguished critic, he is the author of many articles and works of criticism, including *The Novel and the Modern World*.

J. Frank Goodridge is Senior Lecturer in English Literature at St. Mary's College, Strawberry Hill, England.

Albert J. Guérard is Professor of English at Stanford University. His critical studies include books on Robert Bridges, Hardy, Gide, and Conrad, but he is also a novelist, the author of *The Hunted* (1942), *Night Journey* (1948), *The Bystander* (1958), and *The Exiles* (1962).

Arnold Kettle is Senior Lecturer in English at the University of Leeds. He is author of *An Introduction to the English Novel*.

J. Hillis Miller has been Professor of English at Johns Hopkins University since 1963. Among his publications are *Charles Dickens: The World of his Novels, The Disappearance of God: Five Nineteenth-century Writers* and *Poets of Reality*.

Victor Sawdon Pritchett is editor of *The New Statesman and Nation*. He was Beckman Professor at the University of California at Berkeley, and in 1966 was Writer-in-Residence at Smith College. His work includes both criticism and fiction. *The Working Novelist* and *London Perceived* are among his latest publications.

Charles Percy Sanger was long known to Brontë scholars and students only as C.P.S. He gained his special qualifications for studying the legal background of *Wuthering Heights* in the practice of law, and is the author of *Rules and Administration Relating to Wills and Intestaces*.

MARK SCHORER is currently Professor of English Literature, and Chairman of the Department of English at the University of California at Berkeley. He has written many books, including both novels and criticism; among these are studies of Sinclair Lewis and Emily Brontë.

EDGAR E. SHANNON, JR. is the President of the University of Virginia. He was formerly Professor of English at Virginia, and has written books on Chaucer and Tennyson.

ERIC SOLOMON is Associate Professor of English at San Francisco State College. He is the author of *Stephen Crane: From Parody to Realism.*

DEREK TRAVERSI is best known for his studies on Shakespeare. Among his recent works is *William Shakespeare: The Early Comedies.*

DOROTHY VAN GHENT has taught literature at the Universities of Vermont and Kansas, and at Brandeis. She is author of *The English Novel: Form and Function.*

VIRGINIA WOOLF commented extensively on authors and their works in her *Common Reader* essays. One of the most important English novelists of this century, her works include: *The Voyage Out, Night and Day, Jacob's Room, Mrs. Dalloway, To the Lighthouse, The Waves,* and *Between Acts.*

Selected Bibliography

For further reading, students should go first to the complete versions of three studies represented in this volume by selections only. Professor Goodridge's essay is the conclusion of an excellent reading of the novel. Professor Miller's chapter on Emily Brontë in *The Disappearance of God* is one of the most thorough discussions of the religious sources and implications of Emily Brontë's writings. Dorothy Van Ghent's essay is a point of reference for many of the recent studies.

Blondel, Jacques. *Emily Brontë: Expérience Spirituelle et Création Poétique.* Paris: Presses Universitaires de France, 1956. One of the most thorough studies of Emily Brontë in print, combining biography, critical history, and the psychology of poetic creativity.

Ewbank, Inga-Stina. *Their Proper Sphere.* Cambridge: Harvard University Press, 1966. A study of the Brontës in the context of early-Victorian female novelists.

Hafley, James. "The Villain in *Wuthering Heights,*" *Nineteenth-Century Fiction,* Volume XIII, Number 3 (December, 1958). An exaggerated presentation of what Hafley calls Nelly Dean's "viciousness." This essay is a good antidote for the assumption that Nelly represents the author's point of view.

Hatfield, C. W. *The Complete Poems of Emily Jane Brontë.* New York: Columbia University Press, 1941. The poems edited directly from the manuscripts.

Lehman, B. H. "Of Material, Subject, and Form: *Wuthering Heights,*" in *The Image and the Work.* Berkeley: University of California Press, 1955. An attempt to see the novel from the viewpoint of the author.

Lettis, Richard and William E. Morris, editors. *A Wuthering Heights Handbook.* New York: Odyssey Press, 1961. A collection of essays and comments on *Wuthering Heights.*

Ratchford, Fannie E. *The Brontës' Web of Childhood.* New York: Russell and Russell, Inc., 1964. A comprehensive study of the childhood writings, including maps, drawings and facsimiles.

———. *Gondal's Queen.* Austin: University of Texas Press, 1955; New

York: McGraw-Hill Book Company, 1964. An attempt to arrange the early poems in a sequence, recreating what Miss Ratchford calls a "novel in verse" about the kingdom of Gondal.

Spark, Muriel and Derek Stanford. *Emily Brontë: Her Life and Work.* London: Peter Owen, Ltd., 1960. A good biography, followed by separate discussions of the poems and *Wuthering Heights.*

Thompson, Wade. "Infanticide and Sadism in *Wuthering Heights,*" *PMLA,* LXXVIII (1963). Argues that most of the violence in the novel is directed toward infants and children, and that to read it as a love story is to miss Emily Brontë's irony.

Watson, Melvin R. "Tempest in the Soul: The Theme and Structure of *Wuthering Heights,*" *Nineteenth-Century Fiction,* Volume IV, Number 4 (September, 1949). Suggests an interpretation of the novel as drama, organized into a prologue and five acts, with Heathcliff as hero.